BRIDGEWAYS

Group Style

1

Paul Z. Jambor

English Conversation

- Learning English Has Never Been So Easy -

HAKMUN PUBLISHING CO.

Author: **Paul Z. Jambor**

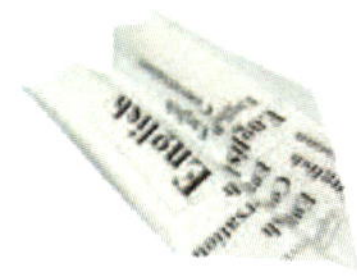

An EFL Book for Korean Learners of English

Bridgeways 1

Group Styled English Conversation

Learning English Has Never Been So Easy

Never has it been so easy to learn English conversation. It only takes a group of learners to utilize this book to get maximum results. That is to say, conversation can only be learned if the language is applied in real use, and what better way to do this than to take part in group conversation in contexts outlined by this book.

First published 2007

Seoul, Korea

http://www.hakmun.co.kr

Price: ₩13,000

ISBN: 978-89-467-8320-1

Foreword

It is important that students form small groups of 4-5 students as they facilitate conversation in the English Classroom. Teachers of English as a foreign language often complain that learners do not engage in oral conversational activities within their classrooms. What they may not realise is that it is often very challenging for learners to do so if the classroom is not set up so as to give the learners the opportunity to converse. It is best to place at least one 'more capable' learner within the group since it gives the other learners the opportunity to improve their conversational abilities. Also, it is a good idea to have learners choose their own groups in order to give them the chance to choose group members they feel most comfortable with. This dramatically increases the chances that learners will actually converse. Perhaps the best method is to pick the more capable learners ahead of time so they can pick 3-4 members they feel most at ease with. This increases the chances for group harmony and the likelihood that the weaker learners will learn from the more capable others.

What is more, this book exposes learners to some instances of 'casual language'. In essence, 'casual language' is language native speakers use in everyday situations. This allows learners to learn not only the English of the English class, but also the English that is used by people in 'real life'. This increases the learners' chances of understanding everyday conversations when travelling abroad.

- Table of Contents -

Supplementary Materials

Unit 1 Getting to Know One Another

To Be – Singular/Plural, Simple Present and the Interrogative

1 Introductions

Work in groups of 4-5 students, as is shown in the pictures below. It is best if all group members can look each other in the eyes. It is important to form groups as it encourages conversation. Now, introduce yourselves to each other. Use the conversations below as models. Substitute the underlined sections.

English Class English

T1

A) What's your name?
B) My name is Jeff Dalton.

A) Where are you from?
B) I'm from Japan.

A) How old are you?
B) I'm 23 years old.

A) What's your hobby?
B) -I like (verb + ing) (noun).
-I like playing baseball.
-I like watching TV.

A) How are you?
B) I'm fine thank you and you?

A) Good morning. How are you?
B) Good. How are you?

A) Good day John.
B) Good Day Kathy.

A) Good afternoon.
B) Good afternoon.

Greetings

Good Morning | Good Day | Good Evening | Good Night

Casual Language

T2

A) Michael Jordan. (Handshake)
B) Paul Henderson.

A) What's your age?
B) 35.

A) What's up?
B) Not much?

A) How's it going?
B) -Pretty good.
-Not bad.

A) What's happening?
B) Not Much.

A) Are you from around here?
B) Yep! / No! I'm from Atlanta.

A) Are you into hockey?
B) -Yeah! I am. / Sure!
-No, not really. I'm into baseball.
-Not really. I'm a couch potato.

A) Do you like Britney Spears?
B) Yeah. I like her.

A) Are you into the Beatles?
B) Not really. I prefer Madonna.

It's important to realise that 'casual language' is the kind of language people use in everyday situations. This kind of language use usually puts people at ease with one another and allows for a more relaxing conversation. It's simply the kind of language many people feel most comfortable using. In other words, it's casual conversation.

Grammar Focus

To be

I	am
you	are
he	is
she	
it	
we	are
you	
they	

Possessive Adjectives

my	- my mother
your	- your sister
his	- his father
her	- her cousin
our	- our parents
your	- your brothers
their	- their aunt

(See Unit 2)

Grammar In Context – Substitution Charts

What	is	your	name	?
			hobby	
	are	your/their	names	
			hobbies	

My	name	is	Daniel	.
	hobby		reading	
Our/Their	names	are	Peter and Paul	
	hobbies		reading and running	

what is = what's

T3

What is your name?	My name is Paul.
What are their names?	Their names are John and Peter.
What's your name?	Peter.

2 Conversation Practice

Now, use the above substitution charts to practice the conversations. Remember to substitute the underlined sections. It is important that everyone in the group has an equal chance to speak. Divide your speaking time equally.

Grammar In Context – Substitution Charts

<table>
<tr><td rowspan="2">Are</td><td rowspan="2">you</td><td rowspan="2">into</td><td><u>hockey</u></td><td rowspan="6">?</td></tr>
<tr><td><u>rock music</u></td></tr>
<tr><td rowspan="2">Is</td><td rowspan="2">he/she</td><td rowspan="2">into</td><td><u>basketball</u></td></tr>
<tr><td><u>rap music</u></td></tr>
<tr><td rowspan="2">Are</td><td rowspan="2">they</td><td rowspan="2">into</td><td><u>basketball</u></td></tr>
<tr><td><u>rap music</u></td></tr>
</table>

<table>
<tr><td rowspan="3">Yes,</td><td>I</td><td colspan="2">am</td><td rowspan="6">.</td></tr>
<tr><td>he/she</td><td colspan="2">is</td></tr>
<tr><td>they</td><td colspan="2">are</td></tr>
<tr><td rowspan="3">No,</td><td>I</td><td>am</td><td rowspan="3">not</td></tr>
<tr><td>he/she</td><td>is</td></tr>
<tr><td>they</td><td>are</td></tr>
</table>

I am = I'm	he is = he's	she is = she's
it is = it's	we are = we're	they are = they're
not really = no	are not = aren't	is not = isn't

T4

Are you into basketball? — Yes, I am.
Is she into rap music? — No, she isn't.
Are they into Madonna? — No.

3 Conversation Practice

Practice the example conversations from the substitution charts with your groups.

4 Review Exercise

Now close your books and try to have the same conversations all over again. It is best if you do not open your books when you do this exercise.

5 Practice Exercise

Check the correct sentences.

a) □ Yes, they is. □ Yes, they are.

b) □ What is your names? □ What are your names?

Vocabulary

actually	favourite	hockey	no	reading	to be into
around	good	into	not really	really	what
basketball	happening	music	play	running	yes
couch potato	hobby	name	prefer	sure	your

6 Writing Practice for Reinforcement

Use the words form the vocabulary list and write your own sentences in the space provided below. You may use the previously exemplified sentence formats as models for your sentences. Work in groups.

____

____

____

____

____

____

____

7 Conversation Practice

Use your own sentences from above to generate your own conversations.

8 Review Activity

Complete the following puzzle. Check the 'Vocabulary List' for possible solutions.

Are you into hockey?

ACROSS

1. What's ____________?
5. No. I ________ Madonna.
6. Are ________ into basketball?
9. Are you ______ rap music?
10. Opposite of no.
12. _______ is your name?
13. What is your _______?
14. Not _______.
16. _______ names are John and Peter.

DOWN

1. My ________ is running.
2. No, he ____ not.
3. Opposite of bad.
4. Yes, you ______.
7. Are you into ___________?
8. I'm a couch __________.
11. Same as yes.
15. Yes, I ____.

Check the 'Review Activity Solutions' section at the back of the book for the solution to the above puzzle.

Unit 2 Family and Friends

Do You Have a Sister?

Family Members

Family Tree

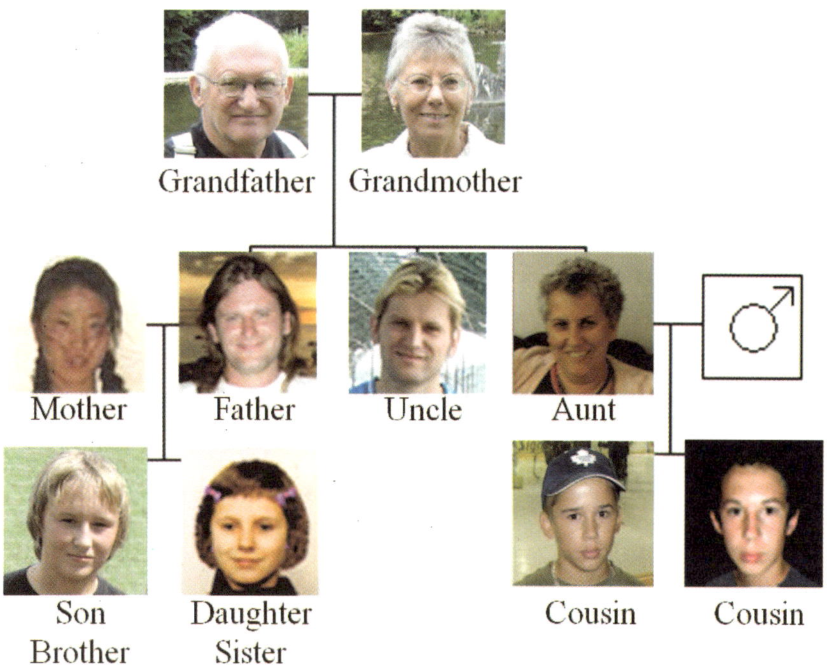

This is a family.
There is a father, a mother, two brothers, one sister and a baby.
The father is into rock music.
The family is into Santana.

Conversation Charts

I/you/we/they do	he/she/it does	Do I/you/we/they…?	Does he/she/it…?

<table>
<tr><td rowspan="4">Do</td><td rowspan="4">you</td><td rowspan="4">have</td><td>a</td><td>sister</td><td rowspan="4">?</td></tr>
<tr><td>any</td><td>brothers</td></tr>
<tr><td>an</td><td>aunt</td></tr>
<tr><td>any</td><td>cousins</td></tr>
</table>

<table>
<tr><td rowspan="2">Yes,</td><td rowspan="2">I</td><td rowspan="2">have</td><td>one</td><td>sister</td><td rowspan="5">.</td></tr>
<tr><td>two</td><td>brothers</td></tr>
<tr><td rowspan="2">No,</td><td colspan="2" rowspan="3">I</td><td>do</td><td>not</td></tr>
<tr><td colspan="2">don't</td></tr>
<tr><td>Yes,</td><td colspan="2">do</td></tr>
</table>

do not = don't

T1

Do you have any brothers?
Do you have a sister?
Do you have any cousins?

Yes, I do.
No, I don't.
Yes, I have two cousins.

1 Conversation Practice

Practice the example conversations from the substitution charts with your groups.

Conversation Charts

What	is	your	mother	like	?
What's			father		
What	are		cousins		
			parents		
What're			grandparents		

She	is	pretty	cool	.
He		very	nice	
They	are	somewhat	laid back	
		kind of	strict	
		pretty much	all right	

what are = what're what is = what's

T2

What're your parents like? They're pretty laid back.
What's your brother like? He's more or less all right.
What's your mother like? She's really wonderful.

2 Conversation Practice

Practice the example conversations from the substitution charts with your groups.

Conversation Charts

Is	your	cousin	married	?
		friend	single	
Are	your	parents	divorced	
	you		married	
Is	your	grandfather	alive	

Yes,	he	is	.
	she		
No,	they	aren't	
Yes, of course			
No,	he	isn't	

T3

Is your cousin married?	Yes, he is.
Is your sister dating?	No.
Is your friend cute?	Yes, she's very cute.
Is your cousin handsome?	No, not at all.
Is your mother pretty?	Sure she is.
Is your grandmother kind?	Not really.

3 Conversation Practice

Practice the example conversations from the substitution charts with your groups.

Is he handsome?

A) Is he your uncle?	B) No, he isn't.
A) Is he your father?	B) No, he isn't.
A) Is he your grandfather?	B) Yes, he is.
A) Is he into hockey?	B) Yes, he is.
A) Is he strict?	B) No.
A) Is he kind?	B) Sure.

Vocabulary

alive	cute	grandfather	like (prep.)	of course	somewhat
all right	dating	grandmother	married	parent	son
any	daughter	handsome	more or less	pretty	strict
aunt	divorced	kind	mother	pretty much	uncle
brother	family members	kind of	nice	single	wonderful
cousin	father	laid back	not at all	sister	

4 Review Exercise

Now close your books and try to have the previous conversations all over again.

5 Practice Exercise

Check the correct sentences.

a) □ What is your parents like? □ What are your parents like?

b) □ Do you have any brother? □ Do you have any brothers?

6 Writing Practice for Reinforcement

Use the words form the vocabulary list and write your own sentences in the space provided below. You may use the previously exemplified sentence formats as models for your sentences. Work in groups.

____

____

____

____

____

____

____

____

7 Conversation Practice

Use your own sentences from above to generate your own conversations.

8 Review Activity

Find words from the 'Vocabulary List' in the word-search puzzle below. Circle the words you find.

```
c s s f k d a u g h t e r
c i o n d i v o r c e d e
r n m r a w n f a m i l y
r g e v t o a u n t f p o
s l w k i n d v d o a a s
h e h a n d s o m e t r t
r r a e g e b r o t h e r
m o t h e r c u t e e n i
g r a n d f a t h e r t c
u a l i i u p r e t t y t
n s i c d l m a r r i e d
c t v e s i s t e r a a a
l p e c o k e c o u s i n
e m o y n e o s c e n m y
```

Check the 'Review Activity Solutions' section at the back of the book for the solution to the above puzzle.

Unit 3 Personal Information

Where are You From?

Personal Information

Her name is Jolan Mecs.

She is from London, Canada.

Her last name is Mecs.

Her first name is Jolan.

Possessive Case

John + 's = John's		John's bag (his bag)
mother + 's = mother's		mother's purse (her purse)

Where do you live?

<table>
<tr><td rowspan="4">Where</td><td>are</td><td colspan="2">you</td><td rowspan="2">from</td><td rowspan="8">?</td></tr>
<tr><td>is</td><td colspan="2">Peter</td></tr>
<tr><td>do</td><td colspan="2">you</td><td rowspan="2">live</td></tr>
<tr><td>does</td><td colspan="2">Angela</td></tr>
<tr><td>What</td><td>is</td><td>your</td><td>father's</td><td rowspan="2">hometown</td></tr>
<tr><td colspan="2" rowspan="3">What's</td><td colspan="2">John's</td></tr>
<tr><td colspan="2">your</td><td rowspan="2">name</td></tr>
<tr><td>your</td><td>mother's</td></tr>
</table>

<table>
<tr><td colspan="2">I</td><td>am</td><td rowspan="2">from</td><td>Seoul</td><td rowspan="8">.</td></tr>
<tr><td colspan="2">Peter</td><td>is</td><td>Canada</td></tr>
<tr><td colspan="2">I</td><td>live</td><td rowspan="2">in</td><td>Tokyo</td></tr>
<tr><td colspan="2">Angela</td><td>lives</td><td>Pusan</td></tr>
<tr><td>My</td><td>father's</td><td rowspan="2">hometown</td><td rowspan="4">is</td><td>Anyang</td></tr>
<tr><td colspan="2">John's</td><td>New York</td></tr>
<tr><td colspan="2">My</td><td rowspan="2">name</td><td>George</td></tr>
<tr><td>My</td><td>mother's</td><td>Angela</td></tr>
</table>

T1

What's your hometown?	Seoul.
Where are you from?	I'm from New York.
Where does Mary's sister live?	She lives in Los Angeles.
Where is Tom from?	He's from London.
What's your father's name?	Andy.

1 Conversation Practice

Practice the example conversations from the substitution charts with your groups.

first name *(given name)* + **last name** *(family name/surname)* = **full name** (name)

full name: George Bush	**first name:** George	**last name:** Bush
Park Ji-Sung	Ji-Sung	Park

What is your last name?

<table>
<tr><td rowspan="2">What</td><td rowspan="2">is</td><td colspan="2">your</td><td>last</td><td rowspan="2">name</td><td rowspan="5">?</td></tr>
<tr><td>your</td><td>father's</td><td>first</td></tr>
<tr><td colspan="2">What's</td><td colspan="2">your</td><td colspan="2">name</td></tr>
<tr><td rowspan="2">What</td><td rowspan="2">are</td><td colspan="2">your</td><td rowspan="2" colspan="2">names</td></tr>
<tr><td colspan="2">their</td></tr>
</table>

<table>
<tr><td colspan="6">Park</td><td rowspan="5">.</td></tr>
<tr><td>My</td><td>father's</td><td>first</td><td>name</td><td>is</td><td>Jonathan</td></tr>
<tr><td colspan="6">June Kim</td></tr>
<tr><td>Our</td><td>names</td><td colspan="3">are</td><td>Andy and Paul</td></tr>
<tr><td colspan="6">Jung-do and Hyun-sook</td></tr>
</table>

T2

What's your last name?	My last name is Park.
What's your first name?	Mira.
What's your father's given name?	His given name is George.
What are your names?	Our names are John and Peter.
What is your cousin's name?	Her name is Mira Lee.
What's his name?	His name is Andrew.

2 Conversation Practice

Practice the example conversations from the substitution charts with your groups.

Are you from around here?

<table>
<tr><td>Are</td><td colspan="2">you</td><td rowspan="6">from</td><td rowspan="2">around</td><td rowspan="2">here</td><td rowspan="6">?</td></tr>
<tr><td>Is</td><td colspan="2">Peter</td></tr>
<tr><td>Are</td><td colspan="2">you</td><td colspan="2">Canada</td></tr>
<tr><td>Is</td><td>your</td><td>father</td><td colspan="2">Japan</td></tr>
<tr><td rowspan="2">Are</td><td colspan="2">they</td><td colspan="2">Mexico</td></tr>
<tr><td colspan="2">John and Tom</td><td colspan="2">Australia</td></tr>
</table>

<table>
<tr><td>Yes,</td><td>I</td><td colspan="2">am</td><td rowspan="2">from</td><td rowspan="2">around</td><td rowspan="2">here</td><td rowspan="6">.</td></tr>
<tr><td>No,</td><td>he's</td><td colspan="2">not</td></tr>
<tr><td colspan="7">Yes, I am</td></tr>
<tr><td colspan="7">No</td></tr>
<tr><td rowspan="2">No,</td><td rowspan="2">they</td><td>are</td><td>not</td><td>from</td><td colspan="2">Mexico</td></tr>
<tr><td colspan="5">aren't</td></tr>
</table>

is not = isn't
are not = aren't

T3

Are you from around here?	Yes, of course.
Are Peter and Matthew from Mexico?	No, they aren't.
Is Mary from Seoul?	Yes, she is.
Is John from around here?	No, he isn't.
Is your family from Portugal?	Yes.
Is your cousin form around here?	No, she isn't.

3 Conversation Practice

Practice the example conversations from the substitution charts with your groups.

Vocabulary

bag	first name	full name	here	last name	purse
family name	from	given name	hometown	live	surname

4 Review Exercise

Now close your books and try to have the previous conversations all over again.

5 Practice Exercise

Check the correct sentences.

a)	□	What's your name?	□	What your name?
b)	□	Where does you live?	□	Where do you live?
c)	□	What her name?	□	What's her name?
d)	□	Are you from Mexico.	□	Are you from Mexico?

6 Writing Practice for Reinforcement

Use the words form the vocabulary list and write your own sentences in the space provided below. You may use the previously exemplified sentence formats as models for your sentences. Work in groups.

____

____

____

____

____

____

____

____

____

7 Conversation Practice

Use your own sentences from above to generate your own conversations.

8 Review Activity

Unscramble the following words in the given spaces.

gab ____________
hree ____________
epusr ____________
mofr ____________
mntoheow ____________
lvei ____________
msanure ____________
anpJa ____________
iMceox ____________
lirsAaaut ____________

See the 'Review Activity Solutions' section at the back of the book for the answers.

9 Review Activity

Complete the following puzzle. Check the 'Vocabulary List' for possible solutions.

Where are you from?

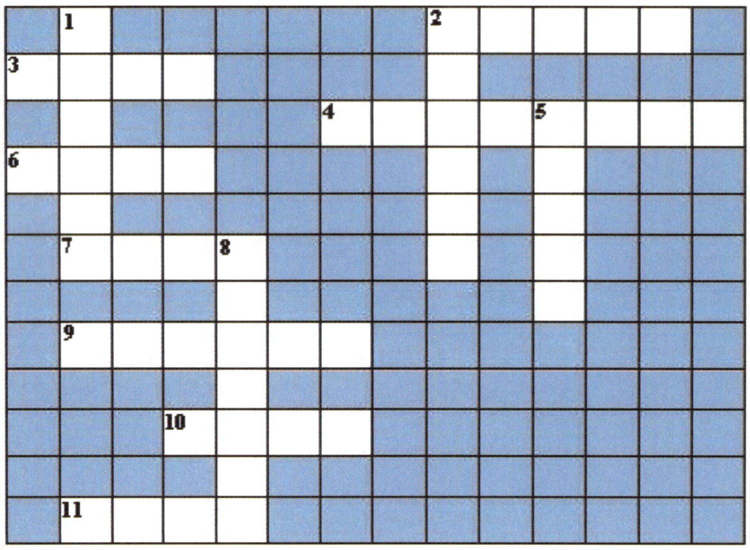

ACROSS

2. What's her _______ name?
3. Where are you ______?
4. My ___________ is Seoul.
6. His ______ name is George Bush.
7. Where ______ she live?
9. Yes, of _______.
10. What's your ______ name?
11. Where does she _______?

DOWN

1. Are you from ________ here?
2. My ______ name is Kim.
5. _______ names are June and Paul.
8. His _________ is Park.

Check the 'Review Activity Solutions' section at the back of the book for the solution to the above puzzle.

Unit 4 I Like Playing Baseball

Present Continuous

He is swimming.

He is swimming.

He loves swimming.

He does not like playing baseball.

He hates playing baseball.

The Verb – To Be

(to be)	(verb + ing)

watch → watching	make → making
do → doing	make → mak (e) + ing → making bake → bak (e) + ing → baking
play → playing	swim → swim + m + ing → swimming

I	am	watching
you	are	playing
he	is	doing
she		taking
we	are	baking
they		swimming

I	am	watching	TV	today	.
You	are	playing	baseball	now	
He/Peter	is	doing	homework		
She/Mary		taking	a shower		
We	are	baking	a cake		
They		making	bread		

T1

I am playing baseball today.
He is doing homework.
They are playing.
We are going home.
Peter is playing the piano.

We are baking bread.
She is taking a shower now.
He is listening to music.
I am coming.
Mary is telling a story.

1 Verbal Practice

Practice the example sentences from the substitution charts by saying them out loud within your group. Substitute the underlined words.

2 Practice Exercise

Check the correct sentences.

a) □ I am watching TV. □ I am watch TV.

b) □ She is doing homework. □ She doing homework.

Grammar Focus – Conjugation of Verbs

I	verb	I	love
you		you	
he	verb + s	he	loves
she		she	
it		it	
we	verb	we	love
you		you	
they		they	

T2

I like playing tennis.
I like watching TV.
She enjoys going shopping.

I love watching hockey.
They love listening to music.
She hates doing homework.

Conversation Charts

I/He/She/We/You/They	like(s)/love(s)/enjoy(s)	(verb + ing)	(noun)	.

I	love	playing	baseball	.
He	loves	doing	homework	
She	hates	listening to	music	
We	enjoy	eating	cake	
You	like	baking	bread	
They	enjoy	taking	a shower	

3 Conversation Practice

Tell your group members about what you like/love and hate to do, using the above formats.

4 Practice Exercise

Check the correct sentences.

a) □ I love play baseball. □ I love playing baseball.

b) □ She hates eating cake. □ She hate eating cake.

c) □ He loves swimming. □ He love swimming.

d) □ I loves watching sports. □ I love watching sports.

Interrogative – Tell Me About Yourself

T3

Do you like playing baseball? -Yes, I do.
-No, I don't.

Does Peter enjoy watching sports? Sure.

Conversation Charts

<table>
<tr><td rowspan="3">Do</td><td rowspan="3">you</td><td rowspan="5">like/enjoy/
love/hate</td><td>watching
(verb + ing)</td><td>TV
(noun)</td><td rowspan="5">?</td></tr>
<tr><td>-playing
-watching</td><td>baseball</td></tr>
<tr><td colspan="2">baseball</td></tr>
<tr><td>Does</td><td>he/she</td><td>doing</td><td>sports</td></tr>
<tr><td>Do</td><td>they</td><td>listening to</td><td>music</td></tr>
</table>

<table>
<tr><td>Yes,</td><td rowspan="3">I</td><td>do</td><td rowspan="5">.</td></tr>
<tr><td>No,</td><td>don’t</td></tr>
<tr><td>Yes,</td><td>do</td></tr>
<tr><td rowspan="2">No,</td><td>he/she</td><td>doesn’t</td></tr>
<tr><td>they</td><td>don’t</td></tr>
</table>

Or

Yes. – Yep. – Sure. – Of course. – Yeah, I do/he does/they do.
No. – Not really. – Not at all. – No way! – Nope. – Not particularly.

5 Conversation Practice

Practice the example conversations by substituting the underlined words.

Casual Language

Do/Does	you/he/she/we/they	(verb)	(noun)	?

<table>
<tr><td>Do/Does</td><td>you/he/she/we/they</td><td>play</td><td>baseball</td><td rowspan="2">?</td></tr>
<tr><td colspan="2">(lazy way – ungrammatical) You</td><td>watch</td><td>hockey</td></tr>
</table>

<table>
<tr><td>Yes,</td><td rowspan="2">I/he/she/we/you/they</td><td>do/does</td><td rowspan="2">.</td></tr>
<tr><td>No,</td><td>don’t/doesn’t</td></tr>
</table>

Or

Yeah. Pretty much.
Never.

do not = don’t   does not = doesn’t

T4

Do you play hockey?	Yes, I do.
Does Tommy listen to music?	Yes, Tommy listens to music.
Do they study English?	Yeah! Sometimes.

6 Conversation Practice

Practice the example conversation from the substitution charts with your group. Model your conversations on the above formats.

7 Review Exercise

Now close your books and try to have the same conversations all over again. It is best if you do not open your books when you do this exercise.

Vocabulary

bake	enjoy	listen to	now	story	today
bread	go	make	shop (verb)	swim	watch (verb)
cake	hate	never	shower (noun)	take	yeah
do	homework	not particularly	sometimes	tell	yep

8 Writing Practice for Reinforcement

Use the words form the vocabulary list and write your own sentences in the space provided below. You may use the previously exemplified sentence formats as models for your sentences. Work in groups.

____

____

____

____

____

____

____

9 Conversation Practice

Use your own sentences from above to generate your own conversations.

10 Review Activity

Find words from the 'Vocabulary List' in the word-search puzzle below. Circle the words you find.

e	n	j	o	y	a	h	l	g
y	e	a	h	w	s	w	i	m
e	s	h	o	w	e	r	s	e
p	t	d	m	a	k	e	t	a
s	o	m	e	t	i	m	e	s
h	d	o	w	c	r	t	n	d
o	a	g	o	h	a	t	e	n
p	y	b	r	e	a	d	v	o
w	b	a	k	e	o	i	e	w
c	a	k	e	s	t	o	r	y

Check the 'Review Activity Solutions' section at the back of the book for the solution to the above puzzle.

Unit 5 The World of Work

What do you do?

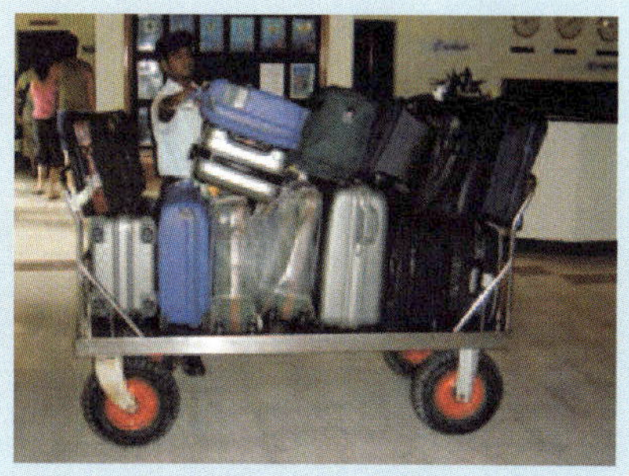

Conversation Charts (To Do)

<table>
<tr><td rowspan="6">What</td><td>do</td><td colspan="2">you</td><td rowspan="6">do</td><td rowspan="6">?</td></tr>
<tr><td rowspan="3">does</td><td colspan="2">Peter</td></tr>
<tr><td rowspan="4">your</td><td>father</td></tr>
<tr><td>mother</td></tr>
<tr><td rowspan="2">do</td><td>parents</td></tr>
<tr><td>friends</td></tr>
</table>

<table>
<tr><td colspan="2">I</td><td>am</td><td>a</td><td>student</td><td rowspan="6">.</td></tr>
<tr><td colspan="2">Peter</td><td rowspan="2">is</td><td>an</td><td>architect</td></tr>
<tr><td>My</td><td>father</td><td rowspan="2">a</td><td>doctor</td></tr>
<tr><td colspan="3">She's</td><td>homemaker</td></tr>
<tr><td colspan="2">They</td><td rowspan="2">are</td><td colspan="2">teachers</td></tr>
<tr><td>My</td><td>friends</td><td colspan="2">unemployed</td></tr>
</table>

T1

What do you do? — I am a lawyer.
What does your father do? — He's a soldier.
What does Peter do? — He's a pilot.
What do Benedict and Arnold do? — They are teachers.

1 Conversation Practice

Practice the example conversations by substituting the underlined words.

Days of the Week

Monday	Tuesday	Wednesday	Thursday	Friday	Saturday	Sunday

Sun	Mon	Tue	Wed	Thu	Fri	Sat
1 Church	2	3	4	5 Swimming	6	7
8 Church	9	10	11	12 Swimming	13	14
15 Church	16	17	18	19 Swimming	20	21
22 Church	23	24	25	26 Swimming	27	28
29 Church	30	31	1	2	3	4

T2

Do you go to church on Sundays?
Do you play baseball on Thursdays?
Do you swim on Thursdays?

Yes, I do.
No, I don't.
Yes, I do.

Conversation Charts

<table>
<tr><td>Do</td><td colspan="2">you</td><td>work</td><td>on</td><td>Saturdays</td><td rowspan="5">?</td></tr>
<tr><td rowspan="2">Does</td><td colspan="2">Agnes</td><td>go to school</td><td colspan="2">during the week</td></tr>
<tr><td rowspan="2">your</td><td>father</td><td colspan="3">work</td></tr>
<tr><td rowspan="2">Do</td><td>friends</td><td>go to church</td><td>on</td><td>Sundays</td></tr>
<tr><td colspan="2">you</td><td>work</td><td>on</td><td>the weekends</td></tr>
</table>

<table>
<tr><td rowspan="2">Yes,</td><td>I</td><td>do</td><td rowspan="5">.</td></tr>
<tr><td>she</td><td>does</td></tr>
<tr><td rowspan="2">No,</td><td>he</td><td>doesn't</td></tr>
<tr><td>they</td><td>don't</td></tr>
<tr><td colspan="3">No</td></tr>
</table>

T3

Do you go to school during the weekdays?	Yes, I do.
Does your family go to church on Sundays?	No.
Do your friends go to school?	No. They work.
Does your sister work?	No. She's a student.

2 Conversation Practice

Practice the example conversations by substituting the underlined words.

Conversation Charts

<table>
<tr><td rowspan="2">Where</td><td>does</td><td>your</td><td colspan="2">father</td><td colspan="2">work</td><td rowspan="5">?</td></tr>
<tr><td>do</td><td colspan="3">you</td><td colspan="2">go to school</td></tr>
<tr><td rowspan="3">What</td><td>school</td><td>do</td><td colspan="2">you</td><td>go</td><td>to</td></tr>
<tr><td>company</td><td rowspan="2">does</td><td rowspan="2">your</td><td>father</td><td>work</td><td>for</td></tr>
<tr><td>university</td><td>sister</td><td colspan="2">attend</td></tr>
</table>

<table>
<tr><td>My</td><td>father</td><td>works</td><td rowspan="2">in</td><td>Canada</td><td rowspan="5">.</td></tr>
<tr><td colspan="2" rowspan="2">I</td><td>go to school</td><td>Seoul</td></tr>
<tr><td>go to</td><td colspan="2">Seoul Girls' Middle School</td></tr>
<tr><td rowspan="2">My</td><td>father</td><td>works</td><td>for</td><td>Samsung</td></tr>
<tr><td>sister</td><td>attends</td><td colspan="2">Suwon University</td></tr>
</table>

T4

Where does your father work?	In Seoul.
Where do you go to school?	I go to school in the U.S.A..
Where does your mother work?	She doesn't work. She's a homemaker.

What company does your father work for?	He works for LG Electronics.
What university does your sister attend?	Seoul National University.

Does your friend go to church on Sundays?	Yes, she does.
Do you work on weekdays?	No, I don't.

3 Conversation Practice

Practice the example conversations by substituting the underlined words.

4 Practice Exercise

Check the correct sentences.

a)	□ Do you school?	□ Do you go to school?
b)	□ Does you friend work?	□ Do your friend work?
c)	□ Do you go to church on Sundays?	□ Do you go church on Sundays?
d)	□ Does she going to school?	□ Does she go to school?

5 Review Exercise

Now close your books and try to have the previous conversations all over again. It is best if you do not open your books when you do this exercise.

Vocabulary

architect	doctor	in	school	to	weekdays
attend	during	lawyer	soldier	unemployed	weekend
church	for	middle school	student	university	where
company	homemaker	pilot	teacher	week	work

6 Writing Practice for Reinforcement

Use the words form the vocabulary list and write your own sentences in the space provided below. You may use the previously exemplified sentence formats as models for your sentences. Work in groups.

7 Conversation Practice

Use your own sentences from above to generate your own conversations.

8 Review Activity

Complete the following puzzle. Check the 'Vocabulary List' for possible solutions.

Where do you work?

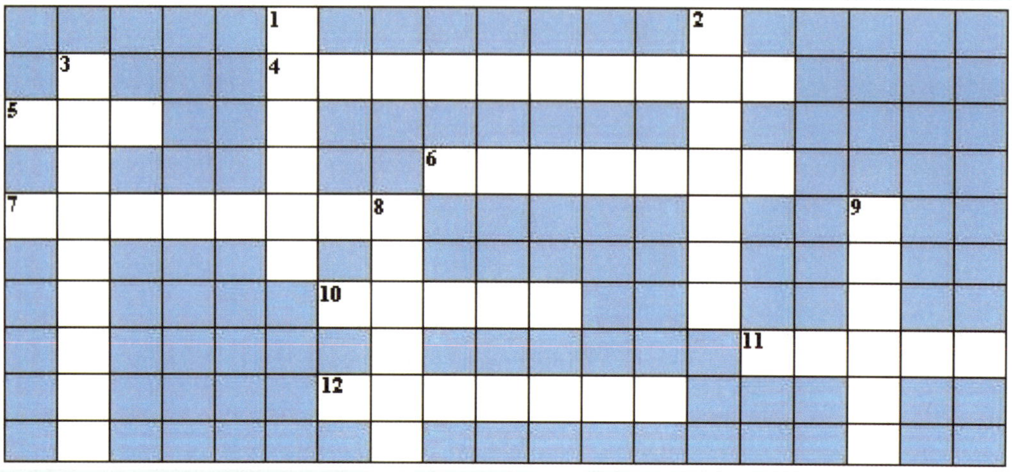

ACROSS

4. My brother attends Oxford _________.
5. My father works ____ Hyundai motors.
6. My sister ________ Oxford University.
7. Does she go to school on the _______?
10. _______ do you go to school?
11. John _______ for Samsung Electronics.
12. What ________ do you work for?

DOWN

1. Do you work _________ the week?
2. My sister does not work. She's a _______.
3. My mother does not work. She's a _____.
8. I go to _______ in Seoul.
9. I go to _______ on Sundays.

Check the 'Review Activity Solutions' section at the back of the book for the solution to the above puzzle.

Unit 1-5 Review

Sentence Building

Unit 1

A Practice Exercise

Check the correct sentences.

a) □ Are you into hobby? □ Are you into hockey?

b) □ Yes, I is. □ Yes, I am.

c) □ He is watch TV. □ He is watching TV.

d) □ What are your name? □ What is your name?

e) □ What is their name? □ What are their names?

B Fill In The Missing Information (To Be)

<table>
<tr><td>I</td><td>______</td></tr>
<tr><td>______</td><td>are</td></tr>
<tr><td>he</td><td rowspan="3">______</td></tr>
<tr><td>______</td></tr>
<tr><td>it</td></tr>
<tr><td>______</td><td rowspan="3">______</td></tr>
<tr><td>you</td></tr>
<tr><td>______</td></tr>
</table>

<table>
<tr><td rowspan="2">My</td><td>______</td><td rowspan="2">is</td><td>Daniel</td><td rowspan="4">.</td></tr>
<tr><td>hobby</td><td>______</td></tr>
<tr><td rowspan="2">Our/Their</td><td>names</td><td rowspan="2">______</td><td>____ and ____</td></tr>
<tr><td>hobbies</td><td>______ and ______</td></tr>
</table>

Unit 2

A Practice Exercise

Check the correct sentences.

a) □ Do you have any sister? □ Do you have any sisters?

b) □ What is mother your like? □ What is your mother like?

c) □ Is your cousin married? □ Married is your cousin?

d) □ My mother is pretty? □ Is my mother pretty?

e) □ They are somewhat laid back. □ They is somewhat laid back.

B Fill In The Missing Information

<table>
<tr><td rowspan="4">Do</td><td rowspan="4">______</td><td rowspan="4">have</td><td>______</td><td>______</td><td rowspan="4">?</td></tr>
<tr><td>any</td><td>______</td></tr>
<tr><td>______</td><td>cousin</td></tr>
<tr><td>an</td><td>______</td></tr>
</table>

<table>
<tr><td rowspan="2">Yes,</td><td rowspan="2">______</td><td rowspan="2">have</td><td>______</td><td>sister</td><td rowspan="5">.</td></tr>
<tr><td>______</td><td>brothers</td></tr>
<tr><td rowspan="2">___,</td><td rowspan="3" colspan="2">I</td><td>______</td><td>not</td></tr>
<tr><td colspan="2">______</td></tr>
<tr><td>Yes,</td><td colspan="2">______</td></tr>
</table>

Unit 3

A Practice Exercise

Check the correct sentences.

a) □ Where is you from? □ Where are you from?

b) □ Where do you live? □ Where lives you?

c) □ My name Angela. □ My name is Angela.

d) □ Are you to around here? □ Are you from around here?

e) □ Yes, I is. □ Yes, I am.

B Fill In The Missing Information

<table>
<tr><td rowspan="4">Where</td><td>______</td><td colspan="2">you</td><td rowspan="2">from</td><td rowspan="8">?</td></tr>
<tr><td>is</td><td colspan="2">______</td></tr>
<tr><td>______</td><td colspan="2">you</td><td rowspan="2">live</td></tr>
<tr><td>does</td><td colspan="2">______</td></tr>
<tr><td>______</td><td>is</td><td>your</td><td>______‘s</td><td rowspan="2">hometown</td></tr>
<tr><td colspan="2" rowspan="3">What’s</td><td colspan="2">______’s</td></tr>
<tr><td colspan="2">______</td><td rowspan="2">name</td></tr>
<tr><td>____</td><td>mother’s</td></tr>
</table>

<table>
<tr><td colspan="2">I</td><td>am</td><td rowspan="2">from</td><td>______</td><td rowspan="8">.</td></tr>
<tr><td colspan="2">______</td><td>is</td><td>______</td></tr>
<tr><td colspan="2">I</td><td>live</td><td rowspan="2">____</td><td>Tokyo</td></tr>
<tr><td colspan="2">______</td><td>lives</td><td>Pusan</td></tr>
<tr><td>My</td><td>______‘s</td><td rowspan="2">hometown</td><td rowspan="4">____</td><td>Anyang</td></tr>
<tr><td colspan="2">______‘s</td><td>New York</td></tr>
<tr><td colspan="2">My</td><td rowspan="2">name</td><td>______</td></tr>
<tr><td>____</td><td>mother’s</td><td>Angela</td></tr>
</table>

Unit 4

A Practice Exercise

Check the correct sentences.

a) □ I am making homework. □ I am doing homework.

b) □ She love playing baseball. □ She loves playing baseball.

c) □ Do you enjoy doing tennis? □ Do you enjoy doing sports?

d) □ Do you playing baseball? □ Do you play baseball?

e) □ He enjoy watching TV? □ Does he enjoy watching TV?

B Fill In The Missing Information

<table>
<tr><td>I</td><td>________</td><td>playing</td><td>baseball</td><td rowspan="6">.</td></tr>
<tr><td>______</td><td>like</td><td>_________</td><td>bread</td></tr>
<tr><td>He</td><td>________</td><td>doing</td><td>homework</td></tr>
<tr><td>She</td><td>hates</td><td>_________ ___</td><td>music</td></tr>
<tr><td>______</td><td>enjoy</td><td>_________</td><td>cake</td></tr>
<tr><td>They</td><td>enjoy</td><td>_________</td><td>a shower</td></tr>
</table>

Unit 5

A Practice Exercise

Check the correct sentences.

a) □ Where do your father work? □ Where does your father work?

b) □ What university do you work to? □ What university do you go to?

c) □ What school attend you? □ What school do you attend?

d) □ Where does your brother study? □ Where does brother attend?

e) □ My mother is homemaker. □ My mother is a homemaker.

B Fill In The Missing Information

<table>
<tr><td rowspan="2">______</td><td>does</td><td>your</td><td colspan="2">______</td><td colspan="2">work</td><td rowspan="5">?</td></tr>
<tr><td>______</td><td colspan="3">you</td><td colspan="2">go to school</td></tr>
<tr><td rowspan="3">What</td><td>school</td><td>______</td><td colspan="2">you</td><td>go</td><td>______</td></tr>
<tr><td>______</td><td rowspan="2">does</td><td rowspan="2">___</td><td>father</td><td>______</td><td>for</td></tr>
<tr><td>university</td><td>sister</td><td colspan="2">______</td></tr>
</table>

Unit 6 What a Wonderful Day

Adjectives – Adverbs

It's Windy

It's not a beautiful day.

The weather is not nice.

It's windy.

It's often windy.

She is not happy.

Grammar In Context – Substitution Charts (Adjectives)

I	am	smart	
You	are	pretty	
He		wonderful	
She	is	beautiful	.
It		awesome	
We	are	happy	
They		sad	

1 Conversation Practice

Practice saying the example sentences from the substitution charts with your groups. Don't forget to substitute the underlined words.

Interrogative Forms – Casual Language

Am	I	handsome	?
Are	you	crazy	
Is	he	all right	
	she	OK	
	Peter	cool	
Are	we	hip	
	they	happening	

Yes,	I/you/he/she/we/they	am/is/are	.
No,		am not/isn't/aren't	

is not = isn't   are not = aren't

T1

Am I wonderful?	Yes, you are.
Is he handsome?	No, he isn't.
Is John amazing?	Yes, he is.

2 Conversation Practice

Practice the example conversations from the substitution charts with your groups. Don't forget to substitute the underlined words.

Adverbs of Frequency (How often?)

Never   Seldom

Sometimes   Often

Frequently   Always

Adverbs of Frequency In Use

The weather	is	sometimes	windy	.
The girl		often	pretty	
The door		always	open	
Peter		never	late	
The students	are	seldom	noisy	
Paul and John		frequently	happy	
Mondays		always	difficult	

T2

The weather is often windy.
The girl is always happy.
Mondays are often difficult.

John is sometimes late.
The train is always noisy.
The weather is seldom rainy.

3 Conversation Practice

Practice saying the example sentences from the substitution charts with your groups.

Interrogative Forms (Adverbs)

Is	the weather	often	rainy	?
	the girl	always	honest	
	the door	never	closed	
	it	so	difficult	
Are	you	never	quiet	
	Mary and Agnes	always	happy	
	Fridays	very	exciting	

Yes,	I/she/it/they	am/is/are	.
No,		am not/isn't/aren't	

T3

Are John and Mary always friendly?	No, they aren't.
Are Sundays always relaxing?	Yes.
Is she always moody?	Yes, she is.

Are Mary and Agnes honest?	Yes, of course.
Are you hip?	Sure.
Is the music often exciting?	Not really.
Is your mother always happy?	Yes, she is.

4 Conversation Practice

Practice the example sentences and conversations from the substitution tables with your groups.

5 Practice Exercise

Check the correct sentences.

a)	□ The students is always noisy.	□ The students are always noisy.
b)	□ Are Mary and John never quiet?	□ Is Mary and John never quiet?
c)	□ The weather is often windy.	□ Often windy the weather is.
d)	□ She is always pretty?	□ Is she always pretty?
e)	□ Is she never honest?	□ She is honest never?
f)	□ Is the music exciting?	□ Music is exciting?
g)	□ The door is always open?	□ Is the door always open?

6 Review Exercise

Now close your books and practice the previous sentences and conversations all over again.

Vocabulary

amazing	difficult	friendly	honest	OK	relaxing
beautiful	easy	happening (adj.)	late	open	very
cool	ever	happy	moody	quiet	windy
crazy	exciting	hip (adj.)	noisy	rainy	

7 Writing Practice for Reinforcement

Use the words form the vocabulary list and write your own sentences in the space provided below. You may use the previously exemplified sentence formats as models for your sentences. Work in groups.

8 Conversation Practice

Use your own sentences from above to generate your own conversations.

9 Review Activity

Complete the following puzzle. Check the 'Vocabulary List' for possible solutions. Also, check adverbs of frequency.

Is it so difficult?

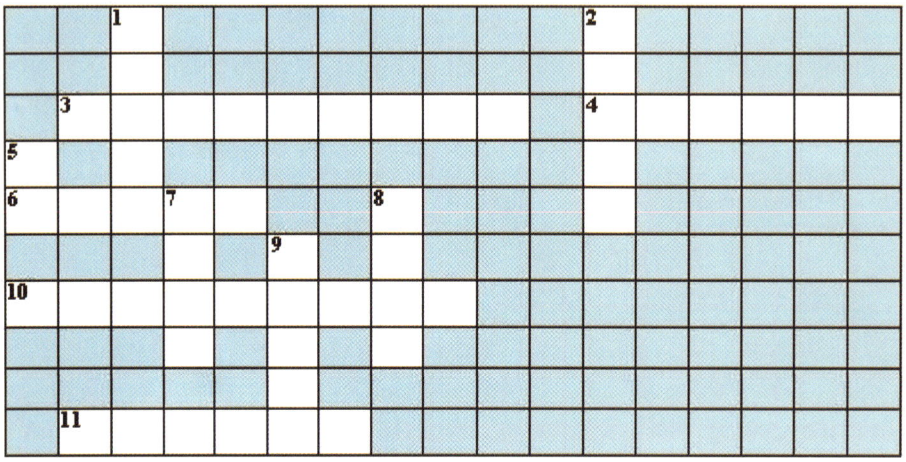

ACROSS

3. Opposite of easy.
4. The girl is _______.
6. The music is _______ exciting.
10. She is _________ sad.
11. Opposite of never.

DOWN

1. Opposite of noisy.
2. Opposite of Sad.
5. It is ___ difficult.
7. Is she ______ quiet?
8. The door is often _______.
9. The weather is often _______.

Check the 'Review Activity Solutions' section at the back of the book for the solution to the above puzzle.

Unit 7 Could You Help me?

Can you/Could you/would you please…?

Could you give me a hand?

A) Can you please give me a hand?
B) Yes, of course. What can I do for you?
A) I would like you to carry this for me.
B) Not a problem.
A) Thank you.

Asking for Assistance (Continuous Conversation)

T1

A) Could you please give me a hand? B) What can I do for you?
A) Would you close the windows? B) Sure. Not a problem.

A) Could you help me? B) OK. What do you need?
A) I need you to hold this for me. B) Sorry. I'm busy.

A) Would you be a sweetheart and give me a hand?
B) Yes, of course. How can I help you?
A) Could you please mail this letter for me?
B) Of course.

Conversation Charts

A)

Can	you	please	give me a hand	?
Could			help me	
Would			give me some assistance	

B)

OK.	How can I help you?
Yes, of course.	What can I do for you?
Certainly.	How may I help you?

A)

I would like you to	carry this for me.
Would you	open the door for me?
Please	give this to Thomas for me.

B)

Not a problem	.
Sure	
All right	

1 Conversation Practice

Practice the example conversations from the substitution charts with your groups. Don't forget to substitute the underlined words.

Offering for Assistance (Continuous Conversation)

A)

Could	I	be	of	any	assistance	?
Can		help	you	in any way		
How	may	I	help	you		
Is	there	anything	I can	do	for you	
What	can	I	do	for	you	
Could	I	offer	you	any	assistance	

B)

Yes.		Could	you	show me the way		?
Sure.	Can	you	tell me	where I am		
Would			hold on to	this bag	for me	
Yeah.	Would		please	open the door	for me	
It's all right.			I don't require any help. (Stop)			
No, thank you. (Stop)						

A)

Sure. Not a problem. Just follow me	.
Of course. You are in Central Park	
Certainly	
Sure	
(No response)	
(No response)	

T2

A) Could I be of any assistance?
B) Yes. Could you please hold this?
A) Certainly.

A) Can I help you?
B) No, thank you.

A) How may I help you?
B) Could you please show me the way to the washroom?
A) Right this way please.

A) Could I help you?
B) Yes. Please mail this letter for me.
A) Sure. No problem.

2 Conversation Practice

Practice the example conversations from the substitution charts with your groups. Don't forget to substitute the underlined words.

3 Conversation Practice

Practice the example conversations from the substitution charts with your groups.

4 Practice Exercise

Check the correct sentences.

a)	□ You please, can you give me a hand?	□ Could you please give me a hand?
b)	□ Can I do for you?	□ What can I do for you?
c)	□ Could you please help me?	□ Help me could you please?
d)	□ How may I help you?	□ May I help you how?

5 Review Exercise

Now close your books and try to have the same conversations all over again.

Vocabulary

anything	close	hold	me	right this way	would
ask	could	hold on to	need	show (verb)	
assistance	door	how	offer	stop	
busy	give	letter	please (adv.)	sweetheart	
can	give a hand	mail	problem	way	
carry	help	may (aux.)	require	window	

6 Writing Practice for Reinforcement

Use the words form the vocabulary list and write your own sentences in the space provided below. You may use the previously exemplified sentence formats as models for your sentences. Work in groups.

____

____

____

____

____

____

____

____

____

____

____

____

____

____

____

____

7 Conversation Practice

Use your own sentences from above to generate your own conversations.

8 Review Activity

Unscramble the following sentences.

hand Could give you me a? ______________________________

may I you How help? ______________________________

can What do you I for? ______________________________

9 Review Activity

Find words from the 'Vocabulary List' in the word search puzzle below. Circle the words you find.

a c a r r y o f f e r
s h o w b u s y a s k
s o s p l e a s e l w
i w r c e l m c p l a
s w e e t h e a r t y
t o q p t o p n o m t
a u u h e l p y b t m
n l i f r d u t l s a
c d r o n a m h e d y
e m e b e e a i m o p
c l o s e w i n d o w
c o u l d y l g o r e

Check the 'Review Activity Solutions' section at the back of the book for the solution to the above puzzle.

Unit 8 Where is the Juice?

Prepositions – Singular/Plural – Numbers (1-10)

Preposition Diagrams

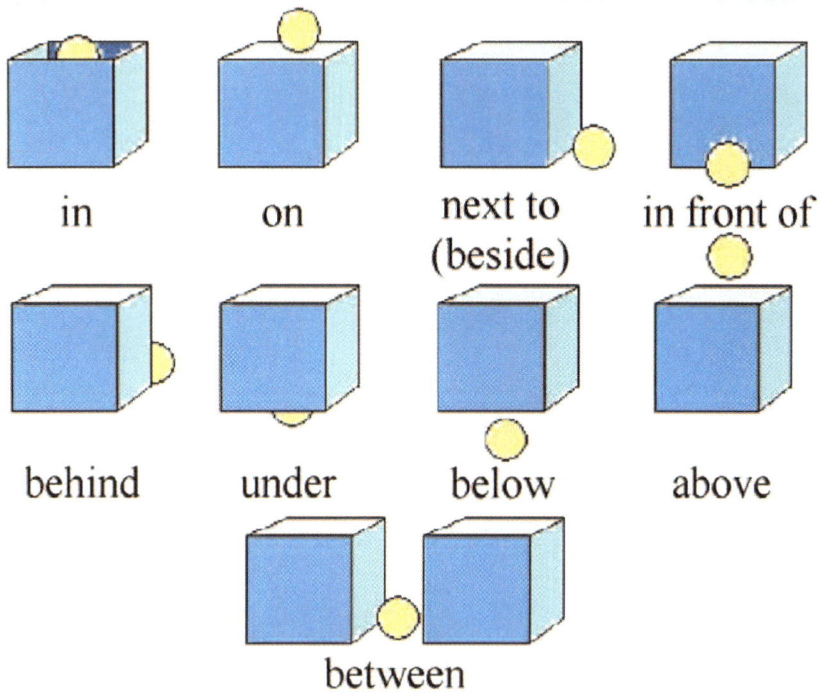

Conversation Chart

The	coffee	is	<u>on</u>	the	<u>table</u>	.
The	boys	are	<u>next to</u>		<u>house</u>	
I		am	<u>in</u>		<u>car</u>	
We		are	<u>under</u>		<u>bed</u>	
He		is	<u>between</u>		<u>trees</u>	
They		are	<u>behind</u>	a	<u>wall</u>	
The	car	is	<u>in</u>	the	<u>garage</u>	

a/an = one (1)

T1

The bus is in front of the house.
The girl is under the tree.
The dog is in the room.
I am on the bed.
The car is in the garage.

The taxi is next to the bus.
They are in the car.
She is between the car and the tree.
Peter is on the train.
The boy is beside the bus.

There are two cups.

Are the cups on the house?

No, they aren't.

The cups are on the table.

There are two cups on the table.

1 Conversation Practice

Practice saying the example sentences from the substitution charts with your groups.

Numbers (1-10)

1 – one	2 – two	3 – three	4 – four	5 – five
6 – six	7 – seven	8 – eight	9 – nine	10 – ten

Singular		Plural	
One table	***One egg***	***Two Tables***	***Three eggs***

Interrogative Forms (Prepositions)

<table>
<tr><td>Is</td><td>the</td><td>car</td><td>in</td><td rowspan="2">the</td><td>garage</td><td rowspan="7">?</td></tr>
<tr><td>Are</td><td>five</td><td>cards</td><td>on</td><td>table</td></tr>
<tr><td colspan="2">Are</td><td>you</td><td colspan="3">in bed</td></tr>
<tr><td colspan="2">Is</td><td>he</td><td>in</td><td>the</td><td>house</td></tr>
<tr><td>Is</td><td>the</td><td>house</td><td colspan="3">on fire</td></tr>
<tr><td>Are</td><td>six</td><td>students</td><td>on</td><td rowspan="2">the</td><td>bus</td></tr>
<tr><td>Is</td><td>the</td><td>dog</td><td>in</td><td>cage</td></tr>
</table>

<table>
<tr><td rowspan="4">Yes,</td><td>the</td><td>car</td><td>is</td><td>in</td><td rowspan="2">the</td><td>garage</td><td rowspan="7">.</td></tr>
<tr><td>five</td><td>cards</td><td>are</td><td>on</td><td>table</td></tr>
<tr><td colspan="2">I</td><td>am</td><td colspan="3">in bed</td></tr>
<tr><td colspan="2">he</td><td>is</td><td colspan="3">in the house</td></tr>
<tr><td rowspan="3">No,</td><td>the</td><td>house</td><td>isn’t</td><td colspan="3">on fire</td></tr>
<tr><td>six</td><td>students</td><td>aren’t</td><td>on</td><td rowspan="2">the</td><td>bus</td></tr>
<tr><td>the</td><td>dog</td><td>isn’t</td><td>in</td><td>cage</td></tr>
</table>

√ on the bus X in the bus

Casual Response

<table>
<tr><td>Yes,</td><td rowspan="2">I/he/she/we/they</td><td>am/is/are</td><td rowspan="2">.</td></tr>
<tr><td>No,</td><td>am not/isn’t/aren’t</td></tr>
</table>

or

Yes./No.

T2

Is the garage on fire?	Yes, it is.
Are the dogs in the car?	No, they aren’t.
Is the girl between the bus and the car?	No.
Is the train in the station?	Sure.
Is the policeman next to the bus?	Yes, of course.
Is the student in front of the school?	No, not yet.

2 Conversation Practice

Practice the example conversations from the substitution charts with your groups. Don't forget to substitute the underlined words.

3 Review Exercise

Now close your books and try to have the same conversations all over again.

4 Practice Exercise

Check the correct sentences.

a)	□ Is the fire on house?	□ Is the house on fire?
b)	□ Is the table on the coffee.	□ Is the coffee on the table?
c)	□ Are bottles on table?	□ Are the bottles on the table?
d)	□ Is the car in the garage?	□ Is the garage in the car?
e)	□ Are six students the bus on?	□ Are six students on the bus?
f)	□ The girl is next to the tree?	□ The girl next to the tree is?

Vocabulary

bed	car	deck	house	policeman	station	tree
boy	card	dog	in bed	rabbit	table	
bus	coffee	garage	not yet	road	train	
cage	cup	girl	on fire	room	tray	

5 Writing Practice for Reinforcement

Use the words form the vocabulary list and write your own sentences in the space provided below. You may use the previously exemplified sentence formats as models for your sentences. Work in groups.

6 Conversation Practice

Use your own sentences from above to generate your own conversations.

7 Review Activity

Describe the picture with your group.

Where is the girl?
Is she in the car?
Is she on the car?
What is she doing?

8 Review Activity

Unscramble the following sentences.

Are you on the bus?

1) the car the in Is garage? ______________________
2) the students bus six on Are? ______________________
3) on bus the are students Six. ______________________
4) cage the the Is dog in? ______________________
5) fire The isn't house on. ______________________
6) table on The the are cards. ______________________
7) the in garage The car is. ______________________
8) He bus is on the. ______________________
9) dog house is next The to the ______________________
10) are We trees the between. ______________________
11) dog house Is the in the? ______________________
12) under the is The tree girl. ______________________

Check the 'Review Activity Solutions' section at the back of the book for the solutions.

Unit 9 Neighbourhood

Around The Block/Directions

Directions

Right

Left

Straight

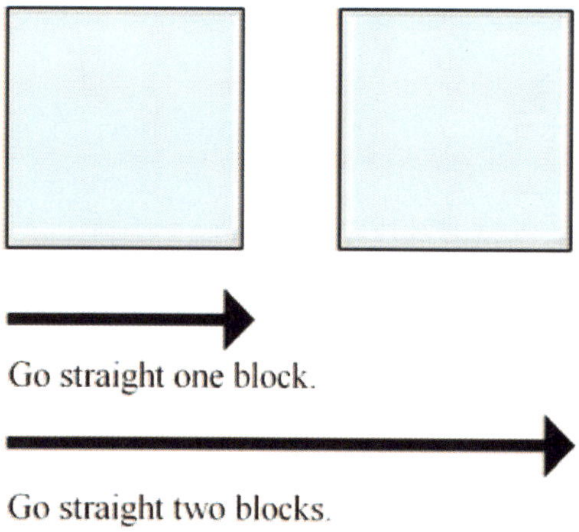

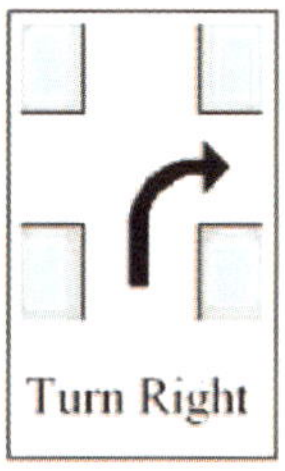

Conversation Tables

Could you	tell me	how to	get to	the bank	?
Would you please	show me	the way to		the bakery	
Do you know	how to	get to		the hospital	
Can you	direct me to			the school	

Yes.	It's right over there on your left hand side.		
Sure.	Go straight one block,	then turn left.	It should be on your left.
Yes.	Go straight two blocks,	then turn right.	Go straight again one block. It should be on your right.
Sure.	Go straight up this street,	then turn left after two blocks.	It should be on your right hand side.
Sorry. I don't know the way./Sorry. I am not from around here.			

T1

A) Could you tell me how to get to the bank?
B) Certainly. Go straight two blocks, then turn right. It should be on your left hand side.

A) Can you direct me to the bus station?
B) Sure. Go up the street 3 blocks, then turn right. Go straight again 4 blocks and it should be on your left hand side.

T2

Directions

A) Can you tell me how to get to the museum?

B) Sure. Go straight two blocks and turn left. Then go straight one block and it should be on your right.

A) Thank you so much.

B) Sure, no problem.

1 Conversation Practice

Practice the example conversations from the substitution charts with your groups.

2 Conversation Practice

Look at the map below and ask for directions to the places on the map. The other members in the group should be able to direct you in the right direction.

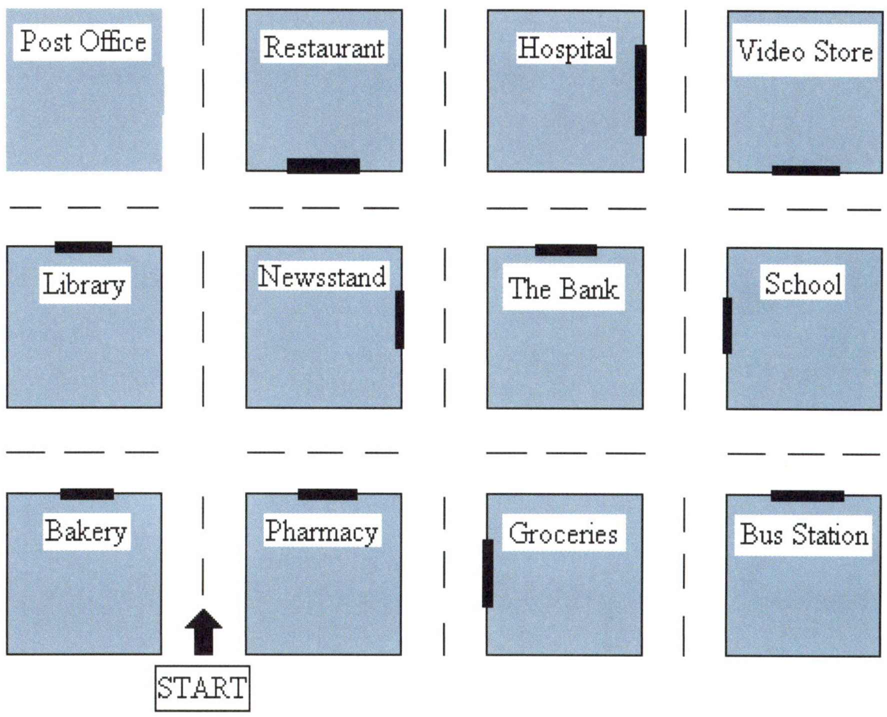

Are you walking or driving?

Driving

Walking

Bicycling (Biking)

How are you getting there?

How are you getting there?
Are you driving/walking/biking?

I am biking/walking/driving.
I'm driving/walking/biking.

3 Conversation Practice

Practice the example conversations from the substitution charts with your groups. Don't forget to substitute the underlined words.

4 Review Exercise

Now close your books and ask your partners about directions to places around your school.

5 Practice Exercise

Check the correct sentences.

a) □ Are you biking? □ Are you bicycle?

b) □ Go straight one block. □ Go straight one blocks.

Vocabulary

after	block	hand	newsstand	start	video store
again	direct (verb)	hospital	pharmacy	straight	walk
bakery	direction	how to	post office	street	
bank	drive	know	restaurant	then	
bicycle (verb)	get to	left (adj.)	right (adj.)	turn	
block	groceries	library	should	up	

6 Oral Practice for Reinforcement

Give names to the various building blocks, then ask your group members for directions to the different places on the map.

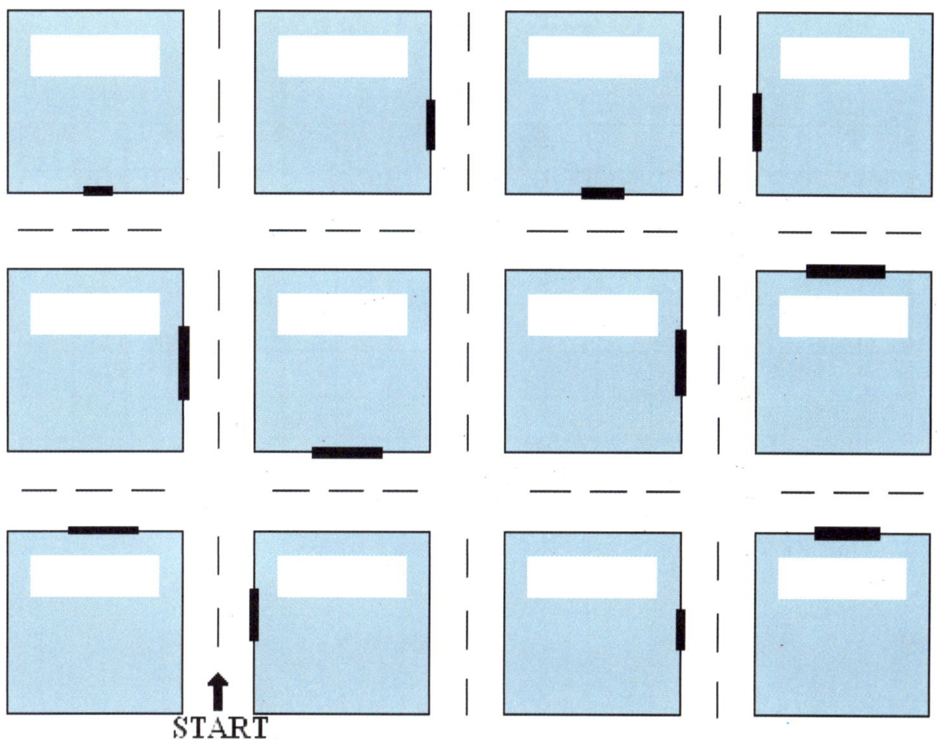

7 Review Activity

Unscramble the following sentences.

tell how me get Can you to bank the to? ______________________

direct to me Can you the station bus? ______________________

block one straight Go. ______________________

8 Review Activity

Complete the following puzzle. Check the 'Vocabulary List' for possible solutions.

Where's the bank?

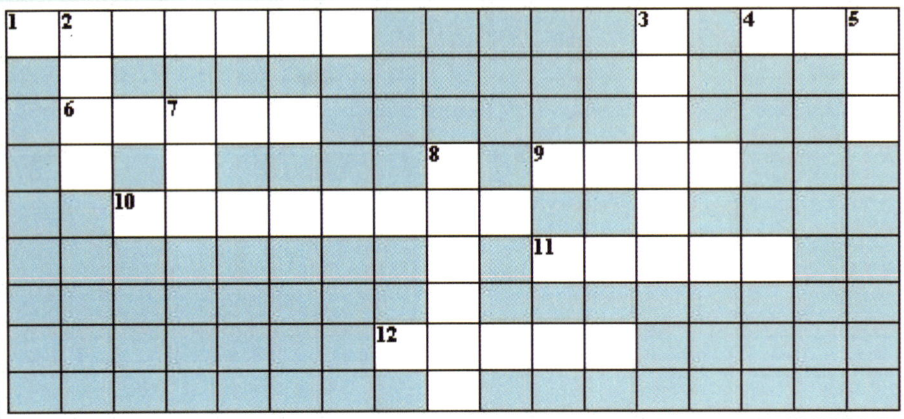

ACROSS

1. It's next to the bus ________.
4. Could you tell me ____ to get to the bank?
6. It's on the ______ hand side.
9. Go straight, __ turn left after two blocks.
10. Go ________ up the street.
11. Turn left ______ two blocks.
12. Go straight one _______.

DOWN

2. ______ right.
3. Can you _______ me to the school?
5. I don't know the _____.
7. Do you know how to __ to the hospital?
8. It _______ be on your left.

Check the 'Review Activity Solutions' section at the back of the book for the solution to the above puzzle.

Unit 10 How Many Eggs?

Countable / Uncountable Nouns

Countable Nouns

How many bananas are there?

There are many bananas.

Countable Nouns

Countable nouns represent those objects or things you can count. For example:

egg/eggs	**tree/trees**	**car/cars**
an egg/two eggs	a tree/two trees	a car/three cars
pear/pears	**person/people**	**child/children**
one pear/six pears	a person/two people	a child/four children

Conversation Charts (How Many?)

How many	eggs	are	in	the	basket	?
	people				room	
	cars		on		road	
	rabbits		in		cage	

There	are	six	eggs	in	the	basket	.
		four	people			room	
		seven	cars	on		road	
		ten	rabbits	in		cage	

Casual Response

One/Two/Three …

T1

How many eggs are in the fridge?	There are six eggs in the fridge.
How many people are on the bus?	Ten.
How many rabbits are next to the dog?	There are six rabbits next to the dog.
How many children are in the room?	Nine.
How many policemen are on the road?	Seven.
How many people are on the train?	There are ten people on the train.
How many pens are in your pocket?	One.
How many teachers are in the school?	Eight.
How many cakes are on the table?	None.

1 Conversation Practice

Practice the example conversations from the substitution charts with your groups.

Uncountable Nouns

Uncountable nouns represent those objects or things you can not count unless a unit of measurement is attached to them. For example:

water	**bread**	**milk**
a litre of water	a loaf of bread	a carton of milk
money	**butter**	**wood**
a wallet full of money	a tub of butter	a pile of wood
honey	**juice**	**flour**
a jar of honey	a bottle of juice	a bag of flour
garbage	**music**	**groceries**
a bin of garbage	one hour of music	a bag of groceries

One Pack of Butter

A) Is there any butter in the fridge?

B) Yes there is.

A) How much butter is there?

B) One pack.

How much?

<table>
<tr><td rowspan="4">How much</td><td>water</td><td rowspan="4">is</td><td rowspan="2">in</td><td rowspan="4">the</td><td>bowl</td><td rowspan="4">?</td></tr>
<tr><td>money</td><td>wallet</td></tr>
<tr><td>butter</td><td>on</td><td>table</td></tr>
<tr><td>milk</td><td>in</td><td>fridge</td></tr>
</table>

<table>
<tr><td rowspan="4">There</td><td>are</td><td>six litres of</td><td>water</td><td rowspan="2">in</td><td rowspan="4">the</td><td>bowl</td><td rowspan="4">.</td></tr>
<tr><td rowspan="3">is</td><td>much/not much</td><td>money</td><td>wallet</td></tr>
<tr><td>one tub of</td><td>butter</td><td>on</td><td>table</td></tr>
<tr><td>one carton of</td><td>milk</td><td>in</td><td>fridge</td></tr>
</table>

Casual Response

Six litres.
Five dollars./Five bucks.
One tub./A tub.
One carton./A carton.

T2

How much money is in your wallet?	Six dollars.
How much water is in the bottle?	There is one litre of water in the bottle.
How much garbage is in the bin?	Not much.
How much music is on the CD?	One hour of music.
How much bread is on the table?	Two loaves.

2 Conversation Practice

Practice the example conversations from the substitution charts with your groups.

3 Review Exercise

Now close your books and try to have the same conversations all over again.

4 Practice Exercise

Check the correct sentences.

a) □ How many water is in the bottle? □ How much water is in the bottle?

b) □ One carton of milk. □ One carton of bread.

c) □ How many eggs are there? □ How many eggs there are?

d) □ Is there any milk? □ Is any milk there?

Vocabulary

bin	carton	garbage	litre	much	pile
bottle	CD	honey	loaf/loaves	none	tub
bowl	child/children	hour	many	of	wallet
buck	flour	jar	milk	pear	water
butter	fridge	juice	money	person/people	wood

5 Writing Practice for Reinforcement

Use the words form the vocabulary list and write your own sentences in the space provided below. You may use the previously exemplified sentence formats as models for your sentences. Work in groups.

6 Conversation Practice

Use your own sentences from above to generate your own conversations.

7 Review Activity

Place the following words into the two categories 'Much and Many'.

money	juice	people	water
wood	butter	honey	litre
hours	milk	flour	eggs
rabbit	music	dog	pear

Much	Many

8 Review Activity

Find words from the 'Vocabulary List' in the word-search puzzle below. Circle the words you find.

```
c h i l d m a n y i a t
l o a f a r m m i l k u
g a r b a g e o e o r b
c h i l d r e n j f a o
p p e r s o n e u l o w
w o o d a c b y i o b l
i e w a t e r f c u u i
b u t t e r e c e r c t
c a r s l i a l e c k r
p e o p l e d e g g s e
u m u c i s m u c h l e
d r h o n e y p e a r s
```

Check the 'Review Activity Solutions' section at the back of the book for the solution to the above puzzle.

Unit 6-10 Review

Sentence Building

Unit 6

A Practice Exercise

Check the correct sentences.

a) □ I am not smart. □ I amn't smart.

b) □ No, you are no. □ No, you are not.

c) □ The weather sometimes windy. □ The weather is sometimes windy.

d) □ Peter and Holly is never quiet. □ Peter and Holly are never quiet.

e) □ Paul happy is. □ Paul is happy.

B Fill In The Missing Information

<table>
<tr><td rowspan="3">Is</td><td>______</td><td>often</td><td>rainy</td><td rowspan="4">?</td></tr>
<tr><td>the door</td><td>never</td><td>______</td></tr>
<tr><td>it</td><td>______</td><td>difficult</td></tr>
<tr><td>______</td><td>Mary and Agnes</td><td>always</td><td>______</td></tr>
</table>

Unit 7

A Practice Exercise

Check the correct sentences.

a) □ Could you mail this for me? □ Could you mail for me?

b) □ Would you close the window? □ Would the window you close?

c) □ Can I offer you any help? □ Can I help offer you?

d) □ Right this way please. □ Right please this way.

e) □ Can I help you how? □ How can I help you?

B Fill In The Missing Information

<table>
<tr><td>Could</td><td rowspan="2">I</td><td colspan="2">____</td><td>of</td><td>____</td><td>assistance</td><td rowspan="4">?</td></tr>
<tr><td>____</td><td colspan="2">help</td><td>____</td><td colspan="2">in any way</td></tr>
<tr><td>____</td><td>may</td><td colspan="2">____</td><td>help</td><td colspan="2">you</td></tr>
<tr><td>Is</td><td>there</td><td>____</td><td>____</td><td>can</td><td>____</td><td>for you</td></tr>
</table>

Unit 8

A Practice Exercise

Check the correct sentences.

a) □ The garage is in the car. □ The car is in the garage.

b) □ Is the fire on car? □ Is the car on fire?

c) □ The cards are on the table. □ The table are on the cards.

d) □ There is two dog in the cage. □ There are two dogs in the cage.

e) □ Is the car in he? □ Is he in the car?

B Fill In The Missing Information

<table>
<tr><td>The</td><td>coffee</td><td>is</td><td>____</td><td rowspan="5">the</td><td>table</td><td rowspan="7">.</td></tr>
<tr><td>____</td><td>boys</td><td>____</td><td>next to</td><td>house</td></tr>
<tr><td colspan="2">I</td><td>____</td><td>in</td><td>____</td></tr>
<tr><td colspan="2">____</td><td>are</td><td>under</td><td>____</td></tr>
<tr><td colspan="2">He</td><td>is</td><td>____</td><td>trees</td></tr>
<tr><td colspan="2">They</td><td>____</td><td>behind</td><td>a</td><td>____</td></tr>
<tr><td>The</td><td>____</td><td>is</td><td>in</td><td>____</td><td>garage</td></tr>
</table>

<table>
<tr><td>____</td><td>the</td><td>car</td><td>____</td><td rowspan="2">____</td><td>garage</td><td rowspan="5">?</td></tr>
<tr><td>____</td><td>five</td><td>cards</td><td>on</td><td>table</td></tr>
<tr><td colspan="2">____</td><td>you</td><td colspan="3">in bed</td></tr>
<tr><td colspan="2">Is</td><td>he</td><td>____</td><td>____</td><td>house</td></tr>
<tr><td>____</td><td>____</td><td>house</td><td colspan="3">on fire</td></tr>
</table>

Unit 9

A Practice Exercise

Check the correct sentences.

a)	□ Turn straight.	□ Turn Right.
b)	□ Go straight two blocks.	□ Go blocks two straight.
c)	□ Turn left after two blocks.	□ Turn left blocks after two.
d)	□ Can you direct to the hospital?	□ Can you direct me to the hospital?
e)	□ I am driving bike.	□ I am biking.

B Fill In The Missing Information

Could ______	tell me	how ____	____ to	the bank	?
Would _____ please	show ____	the _____ to		___ _____	
Do _____ know	_______ to	get ____		the hospital	
Can you	direct _____ to			___ _____	

C Conversation Practice

Look at the map below and ask for directions to the places on the map. The other members in the group should be able to direct you in the right direction.

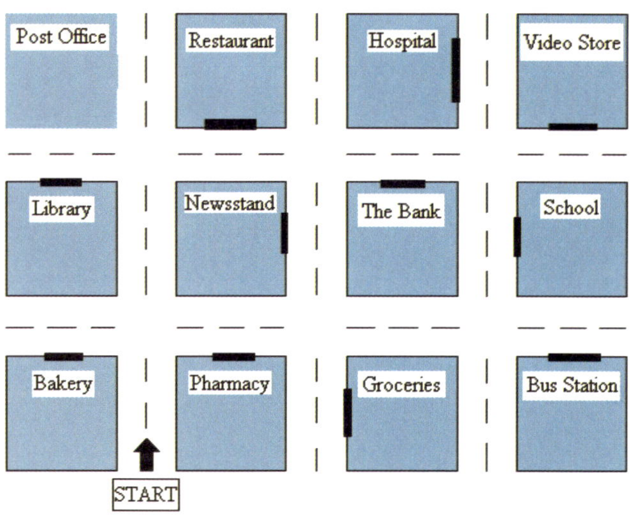

Unit 10

A Practice Exercise

Check the correct sentences.

a)	□ How much cars are on the road?	□ How many cars are on the road?
b)	□ There are an eggs in the basket.	□ There are two eggs in the basket.
c)	□ How many water is in the bottle?	□ How much water is in the bottle?
d)	□ Five buck.	□ Five bucks.
e)	□ A cartons.	□ A carton.

B Fill In The Missing Information

<table>
<tr><td rowspan="4">How ______</td><td>eggs</td><td rowspan="4">______</td><td rowspan="2">______</td><td rowspan="4">______</td><td>basket</td><td rowspan="4">?</td></tr>
<tr><td>people</td><td>room</td></tr>
<tr><td>cars</td><td>on</td><td>road</td></tr>
<tr><td>rabbits</td><td>______</td><td>cage</td></tr>
</table>

<table>
<tr><td rowspan="4">______</td><td rowspan="4">are</td><td>______</td><td>eggs</td><td rowspan="2">______</td><td rowspan="4">______</td><td>basket</td><td rowspan="4">.</td></tr>
<tr><td>______</td><td>people</td><td>room</td></tr>
<tr><td>______</td><td>cars</td><td>______</td><td>road</td></tr>
<tr><td>______</td><td>rabbits</td><td>in</td><td>cage</td></tr>
</table>

Unit 11 Shopping

Currency (Numbers: 11-1,000,000)/Sizes/Kinds of Shopping

Numbers (11-20)

11 – eleven	12 – twelve	13 – thirteen	14 – fourteen	15 – fifteen
16 – sixteen	17 – seventeen	18 – eighteen	19 – nineteen	20 – twenty

Currency ($ - dollar)

$6.00 six dollars $16.00 sixteen dollars

<table>
<tr><td rowspan="5">How</td><td rowspan="5">much</td><td rowspan="3">is</td><td>this</td><td>shirt</td><td rowspan="5">?</td></tr>
<tr><td>that</td><td>hat</td></tr>
<tr><td colspan="2">this</td></tr>
<tr><td rowspan="2">are</td><td>these</td><td>gloves</td></tr>
<tr><td>those</td><td>shoes</td></tr>
</table>

<table>
<tr><td>It</td><td>is</td><td>ten dollars</td><td rowspan="5">.</td></tr>
<tr><td colspan="2" rowspan="2">It’s</td><td>fifteen bucks</td></tr>
<tr><td>one dollar</td></tr>
<tr><td>They</td><td>are</td><td>twelve dollars</td></tr>
<tr><td colspan="2">They’re</td><td>twenty bucks</td></tr>
</table>

this/that **these/those** (See p. 110)

How much is that?

A) How much is that?
B) It's thirteen dollars.
A) Here you are.
B) Thank you.

T1

How much is this cap?
How much is that?
How much are the shoes?

It's fifteen dollars.
It's seventy five bucks.
They're twenty dollars.

1 Conversation Practice

Practice the example conversations from the substitution charts with your groups.

Numbers (20-100)

20 – twenty	21 – twenty one	22 – twenty two	23 – twenty three
30 – thirty	32 – thirty two	33 – thirty three	34 – thirty four
40 – forty	43 – forty three	44 – forty four	45 – forty five
50 – fifty	54 – fifty four	55 – fifty five	56 – fifty six
60 – sixty	65 – sixty five	66 – sixty six	67 – sixty seven
70 – seventy	76 – seventy six	77 – seventy seven	78 – seventy eight
80 – eighty	87 – eighty seven	88 – eighty eight	89 – eighty nine
90 – ninety	98 – ninety eight	99 – ninety nine	100 – one hundred

Sizes

Small **Medium** **Large** **Extra Large**

Conversation Charts

<table>
<tr><td rowspan="5">What</td><td rowspan="5">size</td><td rowspan="3">is</td><td>this</td><td><u>coat</u></td><td rowspan="5">?</td></tr>
<tr><td>that</td><td><u>jacket</u></td></tr>
<tr><td colspan="2">this/that</td></tr>
<tr><td rowspan="2">are</td><td>these</td><td><u>pants</u></td></tr>
<tr><td colspan="2">these/those</td></tr>
</table>

<table>
<tr><td colspan="2">One hundred.</td></tr>
<tr><td colspan="2">Large.</td></tr>
<tr><td colspan="2">It's small.</td></tr>
<tr><td rowspan="2">They're</td><td><u>thirty two.</u></td></tr>
<tr><td><u>thirty four.</u></td></tr>
</table>

T2

What size is this?
What size are those?

It's one hundred.
They're size eleven.

2 Conversation Practice

Practice the example conversations from the substitution charts with your groups.

<table>
<tr><td rowspan="5">Do</td><td rowspan="5">you</td><td rowspan="5">have</td><td rowspan="3">this</td><td rowspan="5">in</td><td>size</td><td><u>ninety five</u></td><td rowspan="5">?</td></tr>
<tr><td colspan="2"><u>eighty five</u></td></tr>
<tr><td colspan="2"><u>large</u></td></tr>
<tr><td rowspan="2">these</td><td>size</td><td><u>one hundred</u></td></tr>
<tr><td>sizes</td><td><u>five and six</u></td></tr>
</table>

<table>
<tr><td rowspan="2">Yes,</td><td>I</td><td rowspan="2">do</td><td rowspan="5">.</td></tr>
<tr><td>we</td></tr>
<tr><td colspan="3">Certainly</td></tr>
<tr><td>No,</td><td>I</td><td>don't</td></tr>
<tr><td colspan="3">No</td></tr>
</table>

T3

Do you have this in size ninety?	Certainly.
Do you have these in size nine?	No.

3 Conversation Practice

Practice the example conversations from the substitution charts with your groups.

Numbers (100-1,000,000)

100	- one hundred	1,000	- one thousand
100,000	- one hundred thousand	1,000,000	- one million

For more detailed information on numbers (100 to 1,000,000,000), see page 111 and 112.

Kinds of Shopping

window shopping online shopping (internet shopping)

Window shopping is when you go to stores to look around, but you do not buy anything.

4 Review Exercise

Now close your books and try to have the previous conversations all over again.

5 Practice Exercise

Check the correct sentences.

a) □ How many is this shirt? □ How much is this shirt?

b) □ Do you have this large? □ Do you have this in large?

Vocabulary

cap	extra large	jacket	pants	small	this
coat	gloves	large	shoes	that	those
currency	internet shopping	medium	size	these	window shopping

6 Writing Practice for Reinforcement

Use the words form the vocabulary list and write your own sentences in the space provided below. You may use the previously exemplified sentence formats as models for your sentences. Work in groups.

7 Conversation Practice

Use your own sentences from above to generate your own conversations.

8 Review Activity

Connect the numbers

One has been done for you as an example.

15	fourteen
17	twelve
20	thirteen
12	one hundred
13	seventeen
100	fifteen
1,000	twenty
14	one thousand

Check the 'Review Activity Solutions' section at the back of the book for the solutions.

9 Review Activity

Complete the following puzzle. Check the 'Vocabulary List' for possible solutions.

How much is this?

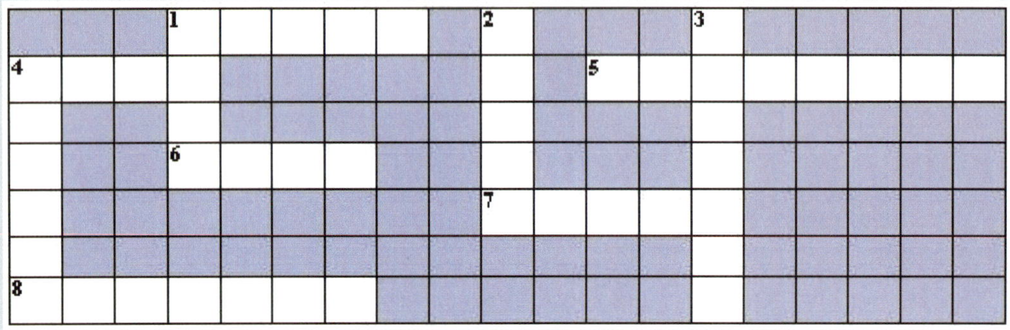

ACROSS

1. How much are ________ pants?
4. How ______ is this shirt?
5. I like window __________.
6. Do you have this in _______ 100?
7. Do you have this in ______ large?
8. 1,000,000

DOWN

1. How much is ______ shirt?
2. Do you have this in _______?
3. It's 6 _________.
4. Do you have this in ________?

Check the 'Review Activity Solutions' section at the back of the book for the solution to the above puzzle.

Unit 12 What Time Is It?

am – pm – quarter – half - o'clock

What time is it?

A) Excuse me? Can you tell me the time?

B) Sure. It's six to four.

A) Thanks.

B) No problem.

Units of Time

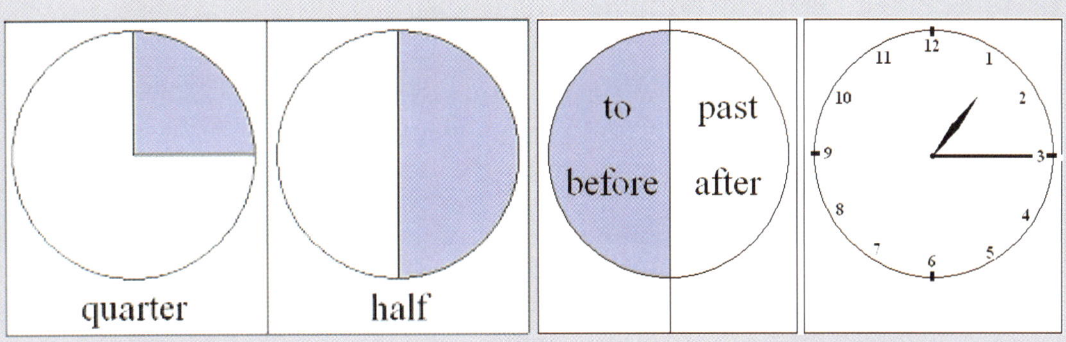

√ half past X half to

am/pm - noon/midnight

am - 00:00 to 11:59
noon - 12:00

pm - 12:00 to 23:59
midnight - 24:00

Examples

quarter to eleven

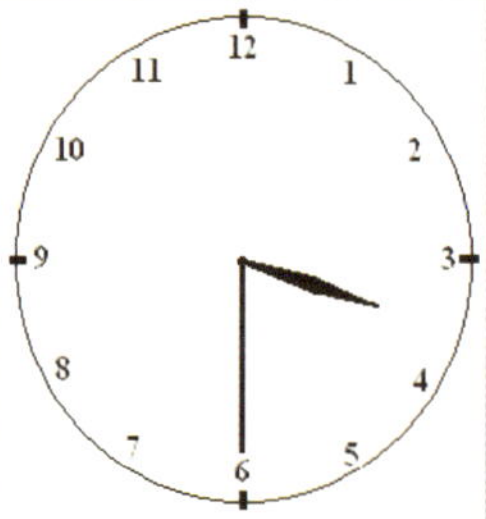

half past three

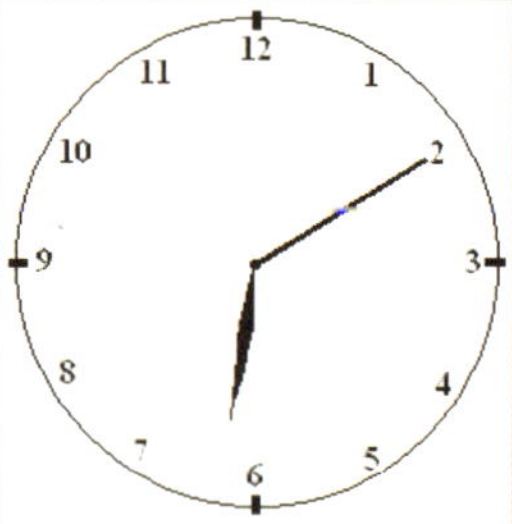

ten after six

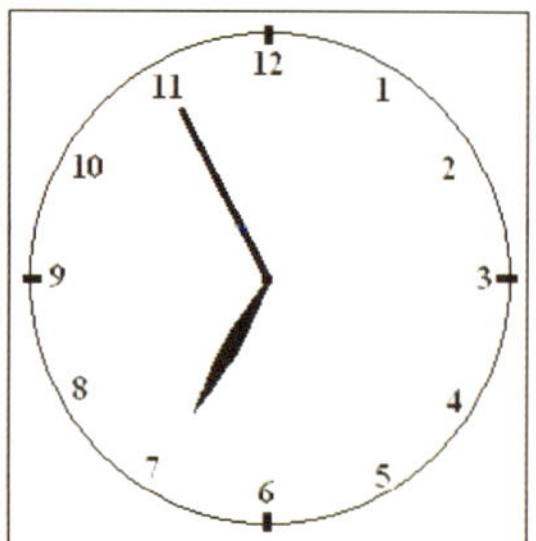

five to seven

Conversation Charts

<table>
<tr><td>Could</td><td rowspan="2">you tell me</td><td rowspan="2">what time it is</td><td rowspan="5">?</td></tr>
<tr><td>Can</td></tr>
<tr><td>Would</td><td>you please tell me</td><td rowspan="2">the time</td></tr>
<tr><td colspan="2">Do you know</td></tr>
<tr><td colspan="3">What time is it</td></tr>
</table>

<table>
<tr><td>Certainly.</td><td rowspan="2">It's</td><td>a quarter after one</td><td rowspan="5">.</td></tr>
<tr><td>Sure.</td><td>a half past six</td></tr>
<tr><td colspan="3">It's ten minutes after one</td></tr>
<tr><td>Sorry.</td><td colspan="2">I don't have a watch</td></tr>
<tr><td colspan="3">Ten to one</td></tr>
</table>

T1

What time is it?
Could you tell me the time?
Would you tell me what time it is?
Do you happen to know the time?

It's half past eleven.
Certainly. It's half past three.
Sure. It's a quarter to four.
Sorry. I don't know.

1 Conversation Practice

Practice the example conversations from the substitution charts with your groups.

Examples

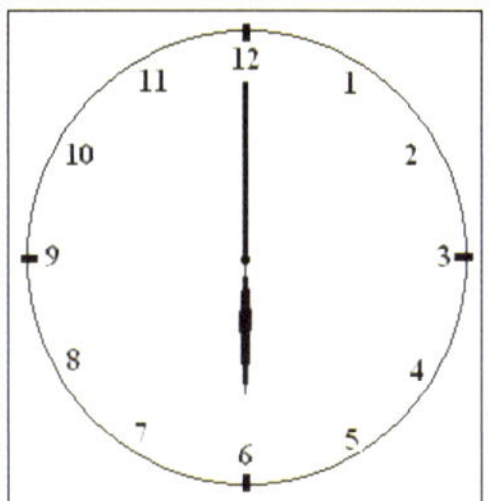
six o'clock

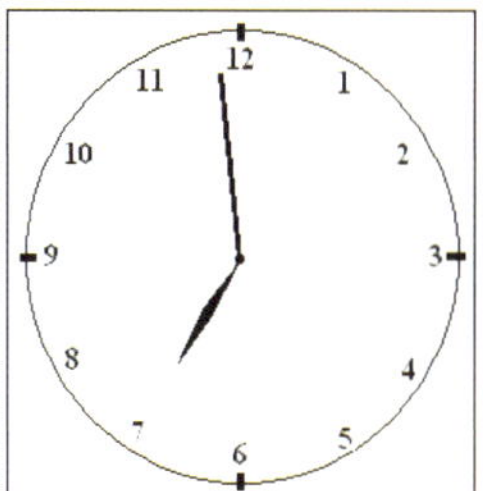
just before seven

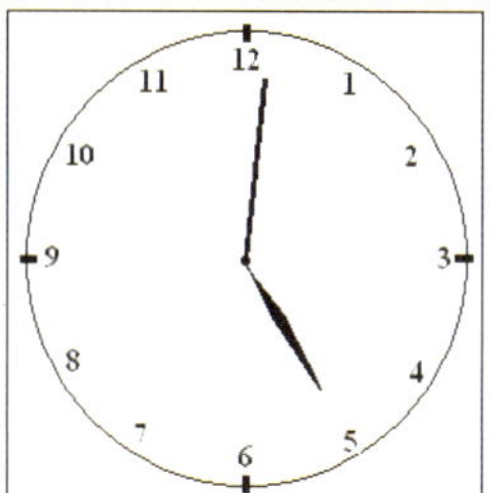
just after five

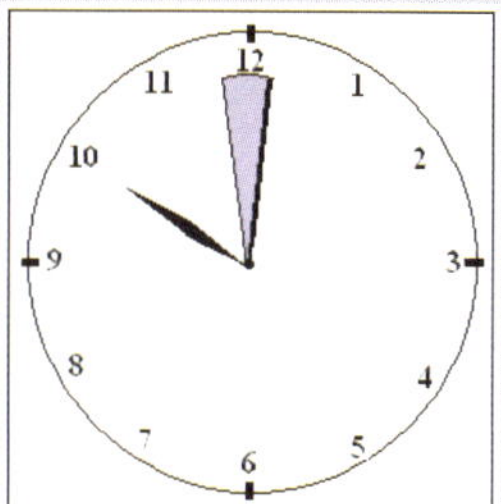
it's around ten

Conversation Charts

Would you mind	telling me	what time it is	?
Could you	tell me	the time	
Do you know		what time it is	
What's the time			

Sure.	It's	six o'clock	.
Of course.		just after eight	
It's around seven			
Sorry.	I don't know the time		

T2

What time is it?
Do you know the time?
Can you tell me the time?
What's the time?

It's just before eight.
It's six o'clock.
It's six.
It's around ten.

2 Conversation Practice

Practice the example conversations from the substitution charts with your groups.

Conversation Charts

What time is it?

It's six pm	.
Just before midnight	

T3

What time is it?
What's the time?
Do you know the time?

Six am.
Just after midnight.
It's six.

3 Conversation Practice

Practice the example conversations from the substitution charts with your groups.

Casual Language

5:20 – five twenty **6:30** – six thirty **2:15** – two fifteen **7:45** – seven forty five

4 Practice Exercise

Check the correct sentences.

a) □ What's time? □ What's the time?

b) □ It's seven past half. □ It's half past seven.

Clock	Watch

Vocabulary

am	just	noon	past	shortly
before	midnight	o'clock	pm	watch (noun)

5 Oral Practice for Reinforcement

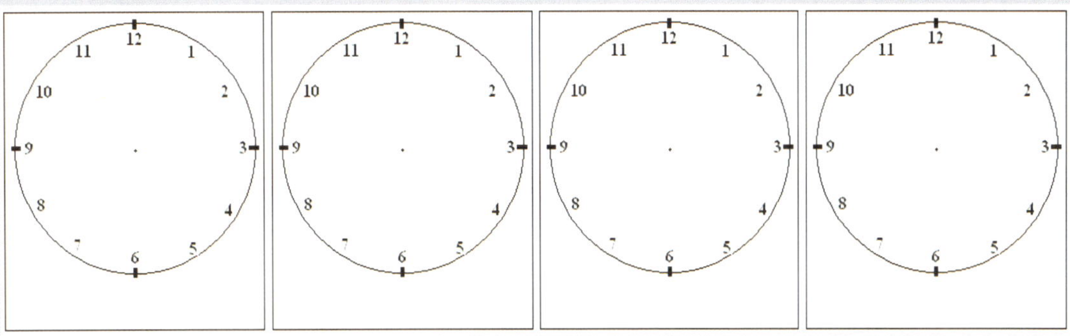

Draw in some times, then ask your group members what time it is in each diagram.

6 Review Activity

Draw in the times into the clocks below. Go by the times written below the clocks.

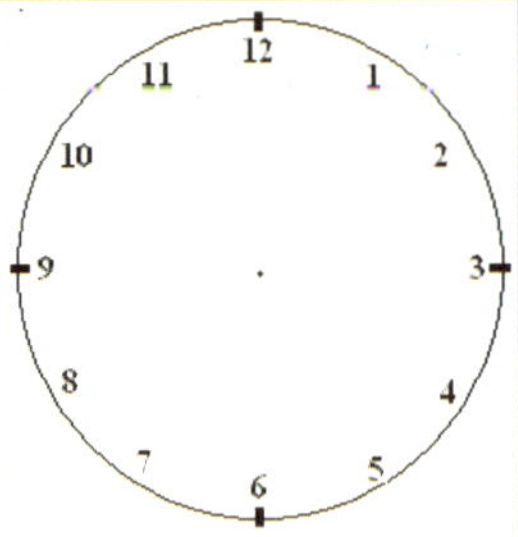

five to seven

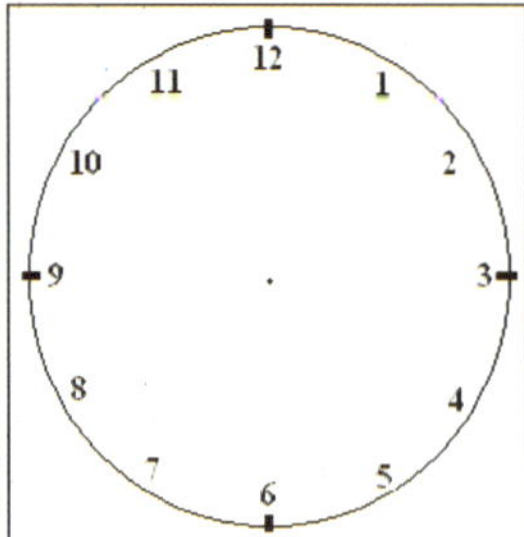

half past three

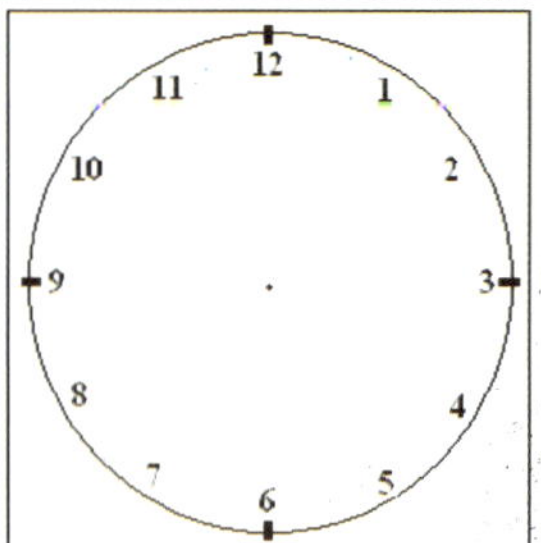

just after five

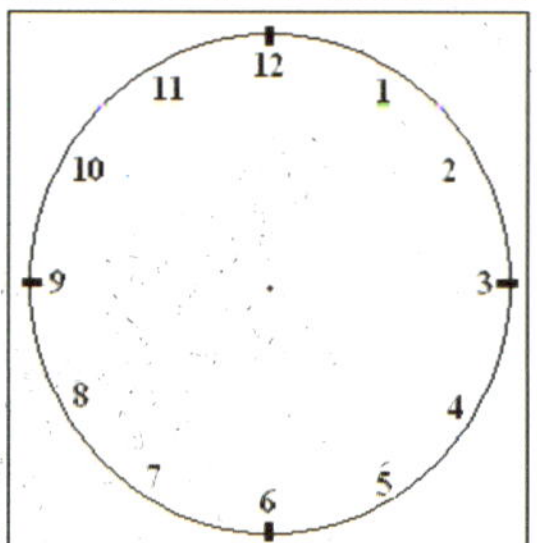

ten after six

Check the 'Review Activity Solutions' section at the back of the book for the solutions.

7 Practice Activity

What time is it?

Connect the times. One is done as an example.

5:30	quarter past six.
6:15	ten past
7:45	it's twelve o'clock
5:59	six after four
12:10	half past five
12:00	ten to three
2:50	three twenty nine
4:06	quarter to eight
3:29	it's around six

Check the 'Review Activity Solutions' section at the back of the book for the solutions.

Unit 13 Now and Then

Simple Past/Long Ago

What did you do last Summer?

Did you attend university last summer?

No, I didn't.

What did you do?

I went to the Philippines with my friends.

It was exciting.

Simple Past (Regular Verbs)

(verb + ed) play + ed study {– y + i} + ed	played studied	I played basketball I studied English

Simple Past (Irregular Verbs)

(no formula)		
run	ran	I ran home
swim	swam	I swam
eat	ate	I ate Italian food
go	went	I went to Hawaii
do	did	I did homework

For more simple past irregular verb forms, go to the back of the book and check the '**Irregular Verbs**' list on page 113.

Conversation Charts

I	watched TV	yesterday	.
She	studied English	last night	
They	listened to music	on the weekend	
You	played baseball	during the summer	

T1

I baked a cake on the weekend.
She watched a movie yesterday night.
We read a book this morning.

1 **Conversation Practice**

Practice the example conversations from the substitution charts with your groups.

Conversation Charts

<table>
<tr><td rowspan="5">What</td><td rowspan="5">did</td><td rowspan="2">you</td><td>do</td><td>yesterday</td><td rowspan="5">?</td></tr>
<tr><td>watch</td><td>on the weekend</td></tr>
<tr><td>Peter</td><td>do</td><td>during the vacation</td></tr>
<tr><td>John and Marry</td><td>study</td><td>last semester</td></tr>
<tr><td>we</td><td>do</td><td>last Friday</td></tr>
</table>

<table>
<tr><td rowspan="2">I</td><td>played</td><td>soccer with my friends</td><td rowspan="5">.</td></tr>
<tr><td>watched</td><td>Titanic</td></tr>
<tr><td>He</td><td>went to</td><td>Australia</td></tr>
<tr><td>They</td><td>studied</td><td>Korean</td></tr>
<tr><td>We</td><td>ate</td><td>at a restaurant</td></tr>
</table>

T2

What did you do this morning?
What did Steve do on Monday?
What did the teacher do two minutes ago?

I took a shower.
He met his friends.
She opened the door.

2 Conversation Practice

Practice the example conversations from the substitution charts with your groups.

Conversation Charts

<table>
<tr><td rowspan="4">Did</td><td rowspan="2">you</td><td>play soccer</td><td>yesterday</td><td rowspan="4">?</td></tr>
<tr><td>go to the movies</td><td>last night</td></tr>
<tr><td>Susanne</td><td>read the book</td><td>last week</td></tr>
<tr><td>she</td><td>play hockey</td><td>during the vacation</td></tr>
</table>

<table>
<tr><td colspan="2">Of course</td><td rowspan="4">.</td></tr>
<tr><td colspan="2">Nope</td></tr>
<tr><td>Yes,</td><td>she did</td></tr>
<tr><td>No,</td><td>she didn't</td></tr>
</table>

T3

Did you play sports when you were young?
Did Jeffery come to soccer practice today?
Did you eat lunch?

Yes, I did.
No, he didn't.
Sure.

3 Conversation Practice

Practice the example conversations from the substitution charts with your groups.

Conversation Charts

When	did	you	start university	?
		he	finish his army service	
		John and Tom	come to class	
		they	leave	

Three years ago.
In 2005.
At half past four.
I don't know.

(at *time*): at 6:00 pm / at 4:30

T4

When did Melanie go to England?
When did the mail arrive?
When did you come home?
When did he cut his hair?
When did France win the FIFA World Cup?

Last summer.
Yesterday morning.
Just now.
A long time ago.
In 1998.

4 Conversation Practice

Practice the example conversations from the substitution charts with your groups.

5 Review Exercise

Now close your books and try to have the previous conversations all over again.

6 Practice Exercise

Check the correct sentences.

a) □ Did you played tennis yesterday? □ Did you play tennis yesterday?

b) □ When did she come home? □ When did she coming home?

Vocabulary

a long time ago	book	eat/ate	lunch	soccer
ago	class	finish	morning	study/studied
army service	come	hair	movie	vacation
arrive	cut	last (adj.)	night	yesterday
at	do/did	leave	run/ran	young

7 Writing Practice for Reinforcement

Use the words form the vocabulary list and write your own sentences in the space provided below. You may use the previously exemplified sentence formats as models for your sentences. Work in groups.

8 Conversation Practice

Use your own sentences from above to generate your own conversations.

9 Review Activity

Complete the following puzzle. Check the 'Vocabulary List' for possible solutions.

When did you finish school?

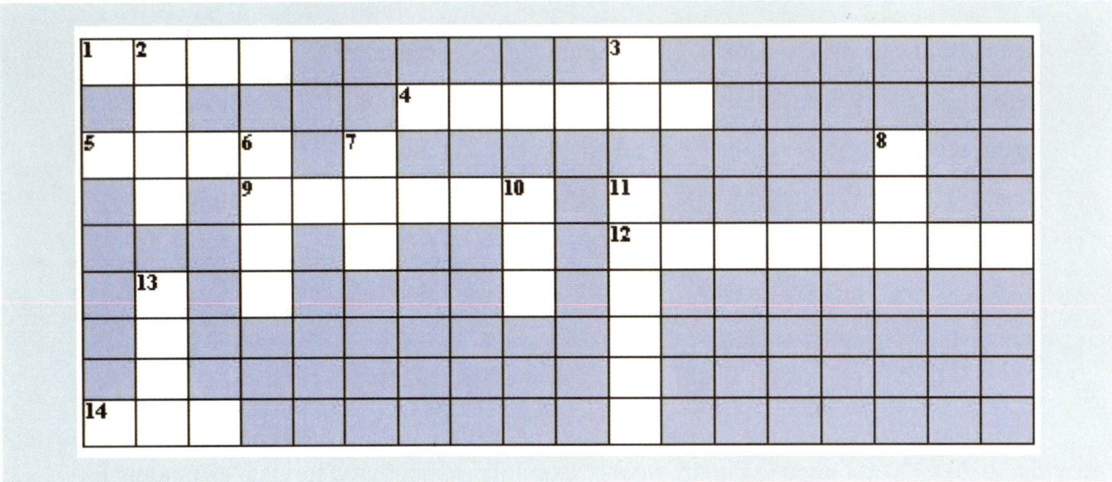

ACROSS

1. Past tense of swim.
4. Did you play hockey _______ the vacation?
5. Past tense of go.
9. I _________ the door five minutes ago.
12. They __________ to music yesterday.
14. They went to Canada two weeks ______.

DOWN

2. Did Susanne read a book last ___?
3. They watched TV ____ the weekend.
6. I _______ a shower last night.
7. I _____ my friends yesterday night.
8. Past tense of run.
10. What ______ you do this morning?
11. We _________ baseball yesterday.
13. I went to Australia a _____ time ago.

Check the 'Review Activity Solutions' section at the back of the book for the solution to the above puzzle.

Unit 14 Future Dreams

What Will …? / In The Future

He will play pool.

He will not play basketball tomorrow.

He'll play pool.

He loves playing pool.

Future Tense

(will + verb) **will + play**	**will play**	**I will play**

I will play baseball tomorrow.

John will study English tonight.

Conversation Charts

What	will	you	do	tomorrow night	?
		Michael		after school	
		John and Marry	play		
		they	do	next week	

I	will	watch TV	.
He		sleep	
They		play tennis	
		do nothing	

I will = I'll he will = he'll she will = she'll we will = we'll they will = they'll

T1

What will you do during the summer?	I will travel to Europe.
What will John do tomorrow?	I don't know.
What will you bring to the party?	I'll bring some snacks.

1 Conversation Practice

Practice the example conversations from the substitution charts with your groups.

Conversation Charts

<table>
<tr><td rowspan="4">Will</td><td>you</td><td>come</td><td>to the party</td><td>on Friday</td><td rowspan="4">?</td></tr>
<tr><td>Michael</td><td>play</td><td>soccer</td><td>this weekend</td></tr>
<tr><td>they</td><td>go</td><td>to Japan</td><td>next winter</td></tr>
<tr><td>you</td><td>help me study</td><td>English</td><td>tonight</td></tr>
</table>

<table>
<tr><td rowspan="2">Yes,</td><td>I'll come</td><td>at 8:00 pm</td><td rowspan="4">.</td></tr>
<tr><td colspan="2">he will</td></tr>
<tr><td>No,</td><td colspan="2">they will not</td></tr>
<tr><td colspan="3">Sorry, I'll be busy tonight</td></tr>
</table>

T2

Will you watch a movie with me?	Sure.
Will you have dinner with me?	Sorry. I'm busy.
Will John come to class?	No, he won't.
Will Manchester United win tonight?	I don't know.

2 Conversation Practice

Practice the example conversations from the substitution charts with your groups.

The Four Seasons

Summer	Fall/Autumn	Winter	Spring

Future Tense (Casual Language)

(to be + going to + verb) **to be + going to + play**	**am/is/are going to play**	**I am going to play**

I am going to play baseball tomorrow. John is going to study English tonight.

Slang Expressions: going to = **gonna/gointa** what are you = **whatcha**

Conversation Charts (Casual Language)

<table>
<tr><td>Are</td><td rowspan="2">you</td><td>going to</td><td>watch TV</td><td>tonight</td><td rowspan="6">?</td></tr>
<tr><td>Will</td><td>come to</td><td>the dinner</td><td>next Wednesday</td></tr>
<tr><td colspan="5"></td></tr>
<tr><td rowspan="2">What</td><td rowspan="2">are</td><td>you</td><td>going to eat</td><td rowspan="3">for lunch</td></tr>
<tr><td>ya</td><td>gonna eat</td></tr>
<tr><td colspan="3">Whatcha</td><td>gointa eat</td></tr>
</table>

<table>
<tr><td>Yes,</td><td>I</td><td colspan="2">am</td><td rowspan="6">.</td></tr>
<tr><td>No,</td><td>I</td><td colspan="2">won’t</td></tr>
<tr><td colspan="4"></td></tr>
<tr><td rowspan="3">I’m</td><td>going to</td><td rowspan="3">eat</td><td rowspan="3">pork</td></tr>
<tr><td>gonna</td></tr>
<tr><td>gointa</td></tr>
</table>

will not = won’t *Slang:* you = ya

T3

Are you going to watch TV tonight?	Of course!
Is Mary going to get married?	No.
Are you gonna come to the meeting?	Nope.
Are ya gonna make dinner?	Sure.
Are you gointa give me some money?	How much?

3 Conversation Practice

Practice the example conversations from the substitution charts with your groups.

4 Review Exercise

Now close your books and try to have the previous conversations all over again.

5 Practice Exercise

Check the correct sentences.

a) □ Will you come to the dinner? □ You will come to the dinner?

b) □ Are you going to eat dinner? □ Are you goingto eat dinner?

Vocabulary

bring	meeting	party	sleep	tomorrow
dinner	next	pork	snack	tonight
fall/autumn	nope	season	spring	win
get married	nothing	slang	summer	winter

6 Writing Practice for Reinforcement

Use the words form the vocabulary list and write your own sentences in the space provided below. You may use the previously exemplified sentence formats as models for your sentences. Work in groups.

____

____

____

____

____

____

____

____

____

____

____

____

7 Conversation Practice

Use your own sentences from above to generate your own conversations.

Will you go travelling this summer?

Yes, I will. I'll go to Thailand.

Are you going to go swimming?

Yes, I will.

8 Conversation Practice

Have a group conversation about the things you plan on doing in the next while. What do you plan on doing tomorrow and in the future to come? Ask and answer.

9 Review Activity

What will you do?

Unscramble the following sentences

Are tonight going watch you TV to? → ______________________

What you are going lunch eat to for? → ______________________

What you tonight do will? → ______________________

pork gonna eat I'm. → ______________________

do Whatcha gonna? → ______________________

play I'm gointa baseball. → ______________________

Will party come to the you? → ______________________

tonight be busy I'll. → ______________________

do What will tomorrow you night? → ______________________

Check the 'Review Activity Solutions' section at the back of the book for the solutions to the above activity.

Unit 15 Food and Cooking

Kinds of Food/Eating Out

Kinds of Food

Italian
pasta

French
crepes

American
hamburger

Korean
kimchi

Chinese
sweet and sour pork

Mexican
chilli

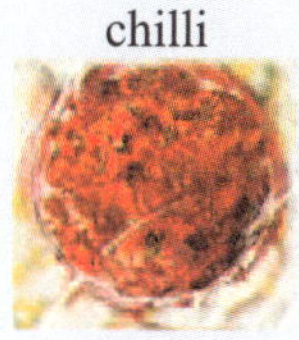

Japanese
sushi

Hungarian
goulash

New Zealand
Meat Pie

A) Do you like Italian food?
B) No, I don't. I prefer Hungarian food. Hungarian food is delicious.

A) What kind of cuisine do you prefer?
B) I prefer Japanese cuisine. I love sushi. It is pretty good.

Conversation Charts

What	kind of	food	do you	like	?
	type of	cooking		prefer	
	kind of	cuisine	does John	enjoy	
		dish	does Tyler	like to eat	
		snack	would you	like me to buy	

I	like	Korean food	.
	prefer	home cooking	
John	enjoys	French cuisine	
Tyler	likes to eat	Hungarian goulash	
Chips			

T1

What kind of cuisine do you prefer?
What type of dish do you enjoy?
What kind of food would you like to eat?

Italian.
I enjoy Mexican chilli.
I'd like to eat ham and eggs.

I would = I'd (See p.110)

1 Conversation Practice

Practice the example conversations from the substitution charts with your groups.

This is delicious bread.

It is Italian bread.

It is a loaf of bread.

My mother baked this bread.

The bread is on the table.

I will eat this loaf of bread.

Conversation Charts

Could	you	recommend	a good	dish	?
			a nice	restaurant	
			a good place	to eat	
			a clean	fast food restaurant	
			a	Chinese restaurant	

Sure.	Crepes are pretty good	.
Certainly.	The Outback Steakhouse is nice	
Hmm…	Little Mother's Kitchen is good	
Burger King		
Yes.	The Mandarin	

T2

Could you recommend a delicious dish?
Could you recommend a nice restaurant?
Could you recommend a good place to eat?

Yes. Try sweet and sour pork.
TGI Friday's is pretty good.
How about KFC?

2 Conversation Practice

Practice the example conversations from the substitution charts with your groups.

Conversation Charts (Casual Language)

What's	a good	Korean side dish	?
	a delicious	Chinese meal	
Where's	a nice	place to eat and drink	
What's	good to eat	around here	

Kimchi.
Sweet and sour pork.
The Hard Rock Café.
Not much.

what is = what's where is = where's (See p. 110)

T3

What's a good Italian dish? What's good to eat around here?	Pizza. Chinese.
Where's a good place to eat? Is the food delicious?	The Mandarin. Sure.

3 Conversation Practice

Practice the example conversations from the substitution charts with your groups.

4 Review Exercise

Now close your books and try to have the previous conversations all over again.

5 Practice Exercise

Check the correct sentences.

a) □ Can you recommend a good dish? □ Can a good dish you recommend?

b) □ What's eat good around here? □ What's good to eat around here?

Vocabulary

buy	cooking (noun)	drink	home	prefer
chips	cuisine	fast food	meal	recommend
clean	delicious	ham	near	type of

6 Writing Practice for Reinforcement

Use the words form the vocabulary list and write your own sentences in the space provided below. You may use the previously exemplified sentence formats as models for your sentences. Work in groups.

7 Conversation Practice

Use your own sentences from above to generate your own conversations.

8 Review Activity

Talk about the food you see below. What kind of food do you think it is?

9 Review Activity

Find words from the 'Vocabulary List' in the word-search puzzle below. Circle the words you find.

```
r c r d d g m n h
e l p r e f e r o
c e b i l h a m m
o a u n i l l s e
m n y k c h i p s
m e c u i s i n e
e a c o o k i n g
n r a c u f o o d
d n o i s t y p e
```

Check the 'Review Activity Solutions' section at the back of the book for the solution to the above puzzle.

Unit 11-15 Review

Sentence Building

Unit 11

A Practice Exercise

Check the correct sentences.

a)	□ How much is this shirt?	□ This shirt is how much?
b)	□ What size this is?	□ What size is this?
c)	□ Do you have this in large?	□ You do have in large?
d)	□ Yes, I have it in medium.	□ Yes, in medium I have it.
e)	□ This is ninety five size.	□ This is size ninety five.

B Fill In The Missing Information

<table>
<tr><td rowspan="4">What</td><td rowspan="4">size</td><td rowspan="3">________</td><td>this</td><td>______</td><td rowspan="4">?</td></tr>
<tr><td>that</td><td>______</td></tr>
<tr><td colspan="2">this</td></tr>
<tr><td>________</td><td>these</td><td>_____</td></tr>
</table>

Unit 12

A Practice Exercise

Check the correct sentences.

a)	□ Could you tell me the time?	□ Could you tell me time?
b)	□ What time it is?	□ What time is it?
c)	□ It's thirty seven o'clock.	□ It's seven thirty.
d)	□ Do know you the time?	□ Do you know the time?
e)	□ It's half past eight.	□ It's eight past half.

B Fill In The Missing Information

<table>
<tr><td>Could</td><td rowspan="2">you ______ ______</td><td rowspan="2">what ______ it is</td><td rowspan="4">?</td></tr>
<tr><td>Can</td></tr>
<tr><td>Would ________</td><td>tell ________</td><td rowspan="2">the ________</td></tr>
<tr><td colspan="2">Do you _______</td></tr>
</table>

Unit 13

A Practice Exercise

Check the correct sentences.

a) □ Did you watch TV yesterday? □ Did yesterday you TV watch?

b) □ What you did yesterday? □ What did you do yesterday?

c) □ What did you this morning? □ What did you do this morning?

d) □ I baseball played. □ I played baseball.

e) □ Yes, I didn't. □ Yes, I did.

B Fill In The Missing Information

<table>
<tr><td rowspan="4">Did</td><td rowspan="2">you</td><td>play ________</td><td>__________</td><td rowspan="4">?</td></tr>
<tr><td>go to the _______</td><td>last night</td></tr>
<tr><td>Susanne</td><td>read __ ______</td><td>last week</td></tr>
<tr><td>______</td><td>play ______</td><td>during the _______</td></tr>
</table>

<table>
<tr><td rowspan="5">______</td><td rowspan="5">did</td><td rowspan="2">_______</td><td>do</td><td>yesterday</td><td rowspan="5">?</td></tr>
<tr><td>watch</td><td>on the _________</td></tr>
<tr><td>________</td><td>do</td><td>during the ________</td></tr>
<tr><td>_____ and _____</td><td>_______</td><td>last semester</td></tr>
<tr><td>we</td><td>do</td><td>last ________</td></tr>
</table>

Unit 14

A Practice Exercise

Check the correct sentences.

a)	□ Will you listen to music tomorrow?	□ Will music listen to tomorrow?
b)	□ What you will do tonight?	□ What will you do tonight?
c)	□ I will baseball play.	□ I will play baseball.
d)	□ Are going to you study English?	□ Are you going to study English?
e)	□ I am going to go to England.	□ I am to going to England.

B Fill In The Missing Information

<table>
<tr><td rowspan="4">______</td><td rowspan="4">will</td><td>______</td><td rowspan="2">do</td><td>tomorrow ______</td><td rowspan="4">?</td></tr>
<tr><td>______</td><td>after ______</td></tr>
<tr><td>______ and ______</td><td colspan="2">play</td></tr>
<tr><td>you</td><td>do</td><td>next ______</td></tr>
</table>

Unit 15

A Practice Exercise

Check the correct sentences.

a)	□ Recommend you a restaurant?	□ Could you recommend a restaurant?
b)	□ Where is a place good to eat?	□ Where is a good place to eat?
c)	□ What kind of food do you like?	□ What kind food do you like?
d)	□ I like food Italian.	□ I like Italian food.
e)	□ French food do you like?	□ Do you like French food?

B Fill In The Missing Information

Could	you	____________	a good	____________	?
			a nice	____________	
			a good place	___ ________	
			a clean	____________	
			a	____________	

Sure.	______ is/are pretty good	.
Certainly.	The ________________ is nice	
Hmm…	___ ______________ is good	
________________		
Yes.	____________________	

Grammar Tips

Affirmative Sentence Format

Josh	***is***	from	Canada	.

↓

Interrogative Sentence Format

Is	Josh	from	Canada	?

Affirmative Sentence Format

Suzanne	***is***	nice	.

↓

Interrogative Sentence Format

Is	Suzanne	nice	?

to be forms & contractions

I am	I'm
you are	you're
he is	he's
she is	she's
it is	it's
we are	we're
you are	you're
they are	they're

to be negative forms & contractions

I am not	I'm not
you are not	you aren't
he is not	he isn't
she is not	she isn't
it is not	it isn't
we are not	we aren't
you are not	you aren't
they are not	they aren't

do (negative forms)	do (negative contractions)
(I/you/we/they) do not	don't
(he/she/it) does not	doesn't

to be (future tense forms)	to be (future tense contractions)
I will	I'll
you will	you'll
she will	she'll
he will	he'll
it will	it'll
we will	we'll
you will	you'll
they will	they'll

Wh… Expressions	Contractions
what is	what's
what are	what're

Wh… Expressions	Contractions
where is	where's
where are	where're

Nearby or Far

Near in Proximity	Farther in Proximity
this	that
these	those

Would - Conjugations and Contractions

I would	I'd
you would	you'd
he would	he'd
she would	she'd
we would	we'd
you would	you'd
they would	they'd

More Numbers

100 – one hundred	101 – one hundred and one	102 – one hundred and two	103 – one hundred and three
110 – one hundred and ten	111 one hundred and eleven	112 – one hundred and twelve	113 – one hundred and thirteen
120 – one hundred and twenty	121 – one hundred and twenty one	122 – one hundred and twenty two	123 – one hundred and twenty three
130 – one hundred and thirty	131 – one hundred and thirty one	132 – one hundred and thirty two	133 – one hundred and thirty three
and so on …			

200 – two hundred	201 – two hundred and one	202 – two hundred and two	203 – two hundred and three
210 – two hundred and ten	211 – two hundred and eleven	212 – two hundred and twelve	213 – two hundred and thirteen
and so on …			

1,000 – one thousand	1,001 – one thousand one	1,002 – one thousand two	1,003 – one thousand three
1,100 – one thousand one hundred	1,101 – one thousand one hundred and one	1,102 – one thousand one hundred and two	1,103 – one thousand one hundred and three
1,110 – one thousand one hundred and ten	1,111 – one thousand one hundred and eleven	1,112 – one thousand one hundred and twelve	1,999 – one thousand nine hundred and ninety nine
and so on …			

10,000 – ten thousand	10,100 – ten thousand one hundred	10,101 – ten thousand one hundred and one	10,200 – ten thousand two hundred
20,000 – twenty thousand	20,200 – twenty thousand two hundred	20,201 – twenty thousand two hundred and one	20,202 – twenty thousand two hundred and two
and so on …			

100,000 – one hundred thousand	101,000 – one hundred and one thousand	110,000 – one hundred and ten thousand	111,000 – one hundred and eleven thousand
200,000 – two hundred thousand	220,000 – two hundred and twenty thousand	222,000 – two hundred and twenty two thousand	255,000 – two hundred and fifty five thousand
and so on …			

1,000,000 – one million	1,100,000 – one million one hundred thousand	1,500,000 – one million five hundred thousand	1,550,000 – one million five hundred and fifty thousand
10,000,000 – ten million	20,000,000 – twenty million	55,000,000 – fifty five million	100,000,000 – one hundred million
150,000,000 – one hundred and fifty million	500,000,000 – five hundred million	550,000,000 – five hundred and fifty million	950,000,000 – nine hundred and fifty million
and so on …			

1,000,000,000 – one billion

Irregular Verbs

Base Form	Past Simple	Base Form	Past Simple
be	was/were	know	knew
beat	beat	leave	left
become	became	lend	lent
begin	began	let	let
bend	bent	light	lit
bet	bet	lose	lost
bite	bit	make	made
blow	blew	mean	meant
break	broke	meet	met
bring	brought	must	had to
build	built	pay	paid
buy	bought	put	put
can	could	read	read
cast	cast	ride	rode
catch	caught	ring	rang
choose	chose	rise	rose
come	came	run	ran
cost	cost	say	said
cut	cut	see	saw
do	did	sell	sold
dig	dug	send	sent
draw	drew	set	set
drink	drank	shake	shook
drive	drove	shine	shone
eat	ate	shut	shut
fall	fell	sing	sang
feed	fed	sit	sat
feel	felt	sleep	slept
fight	fought	speak	spoke
find	found	spend	spent
fit	fit	stand	stood
fly	flew	steal	stole
forget	forgot	stick	stuck
freeze	froze	sweep	swept
get	got	swim	swam
give	gave	take	took
go	went	teach	taught
grow	grew	tell	told
hang	hung	think	thought
have	had	throw	threw
hear	heard	understand	understood
hide	hid	wake	woke
hit	hit	wear	wore
hurt	hurt	win	won
keep	kept	write	wrote

Full Vocabulary List (Unit 1-15)

(Use your English-Korean dictionary and translate the English to Korean)

English	Korean
a long time ago	
actually	
after	
again	
ago	
alive	
all right	
am	
amazing	
any	
anything	
architect	
army service	
around	
arrive	
ask	
assistance	
at	
attend	
aunt	
autumn/fall	
bag	
bake	
bakery	
bank	
basketball	
beautiful	
bed	
before	
bicycle (verb)	
bin	
block	
book	
bottle	
bowl	
boy	
bread	
bring	
brother	
buck	
bus	
busy	
butter	
buy	
cage	
cake	
can	
cap	
car	

English	Korean
card	
carry	
carton	
CD	
child/children	
chips	
church	
class	
clean	
close	
coat	
coffee	
come	
company	
cooking (noun)	
cool	
couch potato	
could	
cousin	
crazy	
cuisine	
cup	
currency	
cut	
cute	
dating	
daughter	
deck	
delicious	
difficult	
dinner	
direct (verb)	
direction	
divorced	
do/did	
doctor	
dog	
door	
drink	
drive	
during	
easy	
eat/ate	
enjoy	
ever	
exciting	
extra large	
fall/autumn	
family	

family members	______________
family name	______________
fast food	______________
father	______________
favourite	______________
finish	______________
first name	______________
flour	______________
for	______________
fridge	______________
friendly	______________
from	______________
full name	______________
garage	______________
get married	______________
get to	______________
girl	______________
give	______________
give a hand	______________
given name	______________
gloves	______________
go/went	______________
good	______________
grandfather	______________
grandmother	______________
groceries	______________
hair	______________
ham	______________
hand	______________
handsome	______________
happening(verb/adjective)	______________
happy	______________
hate	______________
help	______________
here	______________
hip (adjective)	______________
hobby	______________
hockey	______________
hold	______________
hold onto	______________
home	______________
homemaker	______________
hometown	______________
homework	______________
honest	______________
honey	______________
hospital	______________
hour	______________
house	______________
how	______________
how to	______________
in	______________
in bed	______________
internet	______________
internet shopping	______________
into	______________
jacket	______________
jar	______________
juice	______________
just (adverb)	______________
kind (adjective)	______________
kind of	______________
know	______________
laid back	______________
large	______________
last (adjective)	______________
last name	______________
late	______________
lawyer	______________
leave	______________
left (adjective)	______________
letter	______________
library	______________
like (preposition)	______________
like (verb)	______________
listen to	______________
litre	______________
live	______________
loaf/loaves	______________
lunch	______________
mail	______________
make	______________
many	______________
married	______________
may	______________
may(auxiliary)	______________
me	______________
meal	______________
medium	______________
meeting	______________
middle school	______________
midnight	______________
milk	______________
money	______________
moody	______________
more or less	______________
morning	______________
mother	______________
movie	______________
much	______________
music	______________
name	______________
near	______________
need	______________
never	______________
newsstand	______________
next	______________
nice	______________
night	______________
no	______________

noisy	___
none	___
noon	___
nope	___
not at all	___
not particularly	___
not really	___
not yet	___
nothing	___
now	___
o'clock	___
of	___
of course	___
offer	___
on fire	___
open	___
pants	___
parent	___
party	___
past	___
pear	___
person/people	___
pharmacy	___
pile	___
pilot	___
play	___
please (adverb)	___
pm	___
policeman	___
pork	___
post office	___
prefer	___
pretty	___
pretty much	___
problem	___
purse	___
rabbit	___
rainy	___
reading	___
really	___
recommend	___
relaxing	___
require	___
restaurant	___
right (adjective)	___
right this way	___
road	___
room	___
run/ran	___
running	___
school	___
season	___
shoes	___
shop (verb)	___
shortly	___

should	___
show (verb)	___
shower (noun)	___
side dish	___
single	___
sister	___
size	___
slang	___
sleep	___
small	___
snack	___
soccer	___
soldier	___
sometimes	___
somewhat	___
son	___
spring	___
start	___
station	___
stop	___
story	___
straight	___
street	___
strict	___
student	___
study/studied	___
summer	___
sure	___
surname	___
sweetheart	___
swim/swam	___
table	___
take/took	___
teacher	___
tell	___
that	___
then	___
these	___
this	___
those	___
to	___
to be into	___
today	___
tomorrow	___
tonight	___
train	___
tray	___
tree	___
tub	___
turn	___
type of	___
uncle	___
unemployed	___
university	___
up	___

vacation	______________	window	______________
very	______________	window shopping	______________
video store	______________	windy	______________
walk	______________	winter	______________
wallet	______________	wonderful	______________
watch (verb/noun)	______________	wood	______________
water	______________	work	______________
way	______________	would	______________
week	______________	yeah	______________
weekdays	______________	yep	______________
weekend	______________	yes	______________
went/go	______________	yesterday	______________
what	______________	young	______________
where	______________	your	______________
win	______________		

Review Activity Solutions

Unit 1

Across

1) happening
5) prefer
6) you
9) into
10) yes
12) what
13) name
14) really
16) their

Down

1) hobby
2) is
3) good
4) are
7) hockey
8) potato
11) sure
15) am

Unit 2

c	s	s	f	k	d	a	u	g	h	t	e	r
c	i	o	n	d	i	v	o	r	c	e	d	e
r	n	m	r	a	w	n	f	a	m	i	l	y
r	g	e	v	t	o	a	u	n	t	f	p	o
s	l	w	k	i	n	d	v	d	o	a	a	s
h	e	h	a	n	d	s	o	m	e	t	r	t
r	r	a	e	g	e	b	r	o	t	h	e	r
m	o	t	h	e	r	c	u	t	e	e	n	i
g	r	a	n	d	f	a	t	h	e	r	t	c
u	a	l	i	i	u	p	r	e	t	t	y	t
n	s	i	c	d	l	m	a	r	r	i	e	d
c	t	v	e	s	i	s	t	e	r	a	a	a
l	p	e	c	o	k	e	c	o	u	s	i	n
e	m	o	y	n	e	o	s	c	e	n	m	y

Unit 3

gab	bag
hree	here
epusr	purse
mofr	from
mntoheow	hometown
lvei	live
msanure	surname
anpJa	Japan
iMceox	Mexico
lirsAaaut	Australia

Across

2) first
3) from
4) hometown
6) full
7) does
9) course
10) last
11) live

Down

1) around
2) family
5) their
8) surname

Unit 4

e	n	j	o	y	a	h	l	g
y	e	a	h	w	s	w	i	m
e	s	h	o	w	e	r	s	e
p	t	d	m	a	k	e	t	a
s	o	m	e	t	i	m	e	s
h	d	o	w	c	r	t	n	d
o	a	g	o	h	a	t	e	n
p	y	b	r	e	a	d	v	o
w	b	a	k	e	o	i	e	w
c	a	k	e	s	t	o	r	y

Unit 5

Across

4) university
5) for
6) attends
7) weekends
10) where
11) works
12) company

Down

1) during
2) student
3) homemaker
8) school
9) church

Unit 6

Across

3) difficult
4) pretty
6) often
10) sometimes
11) always

Down

1) quiet
2) happy
5) so
7) ever
8) open
9) windy

Unit 7

hand Could give you me a? → Could you give me a hand?
may I you How help? → How may I help you?
can What do you I for? → What can I do for you?

a c a r r y o f f e r
s h o w b u s y a s k
s o s p l e a s e l w
i w r c e l m c p l a
s w e e t h e a r t y
t o q p t o p n o m t
a u u h e l p y b t m
n l i f r d u t l s a
c d r o n a m h e d y
e m e b e e a i m o p
c l o s e w i n d o w
c o u l d y l g o r e

Unit 8

Are you on the bus?

1) the car the in Is garage? → Is the car in the garage?
2) the students bus six on Are? → Are six students on the bus?
3) on bus the are students Six. → Six students are on the bus.
4) cage the the Is dog in? → Is the dog in the cage?
5) fire The isn't house on. → The house is on fire.
6) table on The the are cards. → The cards are on the table.
7) the in garage The car is. → The car is in the garage.
8) He bus is on the. → He is on the bus.
9) dog house is next The to the → The dog is next to the house.
10) are We trees the between. → We are between the trees.
11) dog house Is the in the? → Is the dog in the house?
12) under the is The tree girl. → The girl is under the tree.

Unit 9

tell how me get Can you to bank the to? → Can you tell me how to get to the bank?
direct to me Can you the station bus? → Can you direct me to the bus station
block one straight Go. → Go straight one block

Across

1) station
4) how
6) right
9) then
10) straight
11) after
12) block

Down

2) turn
3) direct
5) way
7) get
8) should

Unit 10

Much or Many?

Much	Many
money	people
wood	litre
juice	hours
butter	eggs
honey	rabbit
water	dog
flour	pear
music	
milk	

c h i l d m a n y i a t
l o a f a r m m i l k u
g a r b a g e o e o r b
c h i l d r e n j f a o
p p e r s o n e u l o w
w o o d a c b y i o b l
i e w a t e r f c u u i
b u t t e r e c e r c t
c a r s l i a l e c k r
p e o p l e d e g g s e
u m u c i s m u c h l e
d r h o n e y p e a r s

Unit 11

Connect the numbers

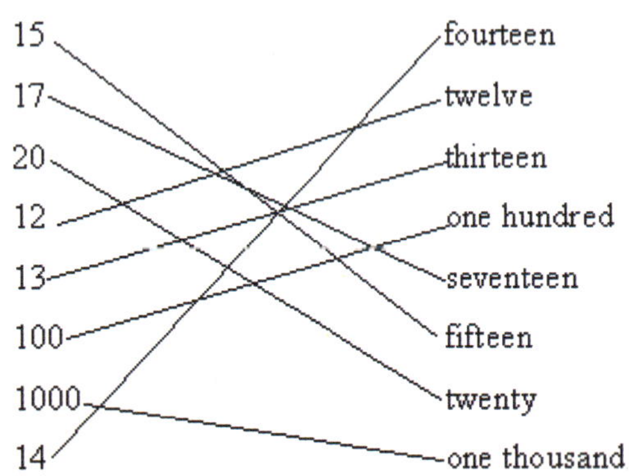

Across

1) these
4) much
5) shopping
6) size
7) extra
8) million

Down

1) this
2) large
3) dollars
4) medium

Unit 12

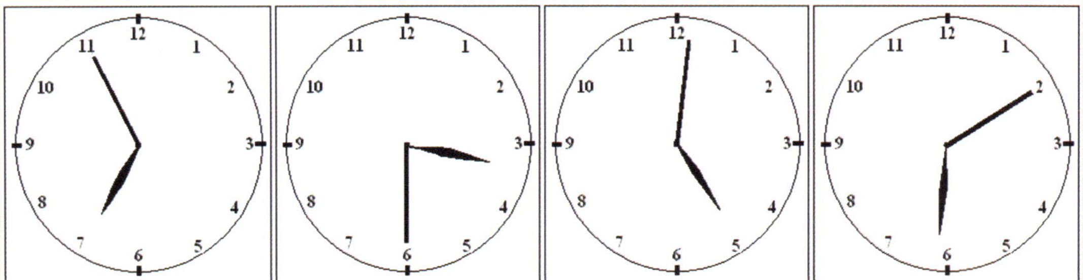

five to seven | half past three | just after five | ten after six

Unit 12

What time is it?

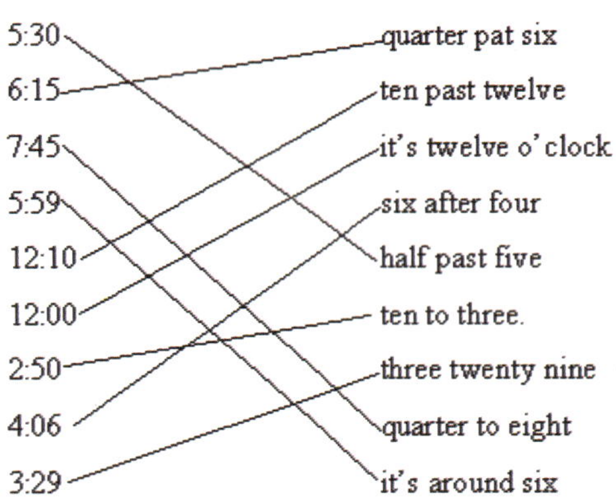

Unit 13

Across

1) swam
4) during
5) went
9) opened
12) listened
14) ago

Down

2) week
3) on
6) took
7) met
8) ran
10) did
11) played
13) long

Unit 14

What will you do?

Are tonight going watch you TV to?	→	Are you going to watch TV tonight?
What you are going lunch eat to for?	→	What are you going to eat for lunch?
What you tonight do will?	→	What will you do tonight?
pork gonna eat I'm	→	I'm gonna eat pork
do Whatcha gonna?	→	Whatcha gonna do?
play I'm gointa baseball	→	I'm gointa play baseball
Will party come to the you?	→	Will you come to the party?
tonight be busy I'll	→	I'll be busy tonight
do What will tomorrow you night?	→	What will you do tomorrow night?
nothing do will I	→	I will do nothing

Unit 15

r	c	r	d	d	g	m	n	h
e	l	p	r	e	f	e	r	o
c	e	b	i	l	h	a	m	m
o	a	u	n	i	l	l	s	e
m	n	y	k	c	h	i	p	s
m	e	c	u	i	s	i	n	e
e	a	c	o	o	k	i	n	g
n	r	a	c	u	f	o	o	d
d	n	o	i	s	t	y	p	e

Paul Z. Jambor

Paul Z. Jambor has 11 years of experience teaching English as a foreign language in Hungary and Korea combined. He has been a foreign language professor at the university level for 6 years now. He has a Master of Arts in Teaching English as a Second/Foreign Language from the UK. Moreover he has undertaken extensive research in the field of English Language Teaching within the context of a Korean university setting, in order to determine the effectiveness of the 'Group Style' approach in teaching English as a foreign language. Through the course of his research Professor Jambor has come to the conclusion that the most effective way of teaching English conversation in the Korean university setting is to teach it in a group setting wherein students have ample means and opportunities to use the language via verbal practice. This method may seem simple in theory, however it is nevertheless tricky to implement in the foreign language classroom since most ES/FL books are not geared toward oral practice. Subsequently, the aim of this book is to provide a suitable classroom setting that encourages students to take active roles in verbal communication. Overall, this book is specifically designed for oral communication practice in a simple and comprehensive manner, so students do not feel overwhelmed with the challenges and pressures of learning a foreign language. In essence, this book is the very thing learners need for oral communicative development. The teaching approach encapsulated by this book is tried and tested by the author. By and large, the book is really the step in the right direction if the aim is to improve oral communicative competence.